Charles W. Walton

BASIC FORMS IN MUSIC

Alfred Publishing Co., Inc., New York

ALFRED PUBLISHING CO., INC.,
75 Channel Drive,
Port Washington, New York 11050

Library of Congress Catalog Card No. 73-81046
ISBN - 0-88284-010-x

Contents

Introduction

"Musical structure is not a set of immutable 'laws' to which music must conform; but rather it is a body of guiding principles gleaned from experience and modified according to circumstances. It is the framework over which the composer drapes his tonal fabric according to his fancy, and the result is always unique because it is individual."

Howard A. Murphy

Throughout the history of music, composers have employed certain fundamental and basic principles of organization and structure which serve as a mold or framework for the presentation of the materials of music—rhythm, melody and harmony. Even though every composition has its own unique and individual qualities, and is the result of the natural development of the composers' ideas, each is based upon the underlying principle of unity and variety, which is achieved by the repetition of musical elements either exact or modified and the presentation of new material. From this need of some kind of plan and order in music, certain basic forms and structures have developed through the years. The focus and emphasis in this book is on these forms themselves illustrated through representative literature with a brief description and analysis for reference and study. Tracing the development of these forms both historically and stylistically is extremely important in the study of music but it is not the purpose or premise of this short collection.

Introduction

Listening is the basis of all musical experience and should be stressed in the study and analysis of these musical forms. It is important that the plan, design, and sequence of the music be considered and presented through an aural awareness and response to the music.

Each chapter of the book presents representative forms within a certain general category of a musical structure and design. Except for the small primary units of form, the musical score of a complete composition is given to illustrate each basic form. These scores offer the opportunity to follow the form in detail as it is heard, and it also offers a variety of selected music literature for further study and the consideration of other elements of music as well—melody, rhythm, harmony, style, texture, etc. In the early stages of the book, the form is quite specific as to phrases, periods, etc. Later on more attention is given to parts and sections and a more detailed analysis is sometimes left to the reader, based upon the earlier experience.

The complete musical score is then followed by a short discussion and analysis of other compositions to illustrate and reinforce the particular form in various contexts, and with various composers and periods. Occasionally, important themes and analytical guides are given for these compositions to aid and guide the listening. Whenever possible, it is, of course, most valuable to listen and analyze with complete scores. Measure numbers are, therefore, frequently provided in the analysis and discussion to facilitate this kind of study. At the end of each presentation of a form, additional suggestions of compositions for extra study and listening are presented with brief "highlights" of the music and an occasional detailed analysis.

CHAPTER 1

Primary
Units
of
Form

The Motive

Almost all music is based on the extension and expansion of a brief group of notes called a *motive*. A motive is a short harmonic, melodic, or rhythmic fragment or figure from which a theme, melody, or entire composition is developed. The following musical examples illustrate some uses of the motive.

1. A four-note pattern serves as the principal motive for the first movement of the Beethoven *Symphony No. 5*. A characteristic feature of the movement, it appears on various scale tones, in contrary motion and in imitation. It also reappears as a prominent rhythmic pattern in the third and fourth movements of the symphony.

Beethoven: *Symphony No. 5,*
First Movement

Allegro con brio

2. A motive may be extended by its repetition on the same scale degrees.

(a) Two groups of sixteenth notes are followed by an exact repetition.

Bach: *The Well Tempered Clavier.*
Book I, Prelude No. 1 in C Major

(b) Respighi repeats a one-measure motive three times in this excerpt.

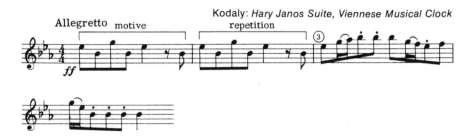

(c) A one-measure motive is repeated, followed by new material to complete the theme.

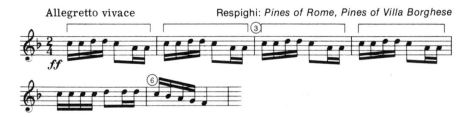

3. A motive is often extended by a repetition on different scale degrees. This kind of repetition is called *sequence* and may be an exact or modified duplication involving melody, rhythm, or harmony, separately or together.

(a) Measure 2 is a melodic and rhythmic sequence of the motive in measure 1. A new motive appears in measure 3, followed by a rhythmic sequence, which completes the four measures. In the second sequence the notes appear in a different order.

Franck: *Symphony in D Minor, First Movement*

Allegro non troppo

(b)́ The theme opens with a five-note motive (measures 1-2), which is repeated in sequence. In measure 6 the motive is extended and "filled in" by a descending scale passage and continues in sequence.

Schubert: *Symphony No. 5 in B♭, First Movement*

Allegro

(c) A four-measure motive beginning with a V₇ chord in arpeggio is repeated in sequence, beginning on F♯ followed by a somewhat altered sequence commencing on A. Each sequence begins a third higher.

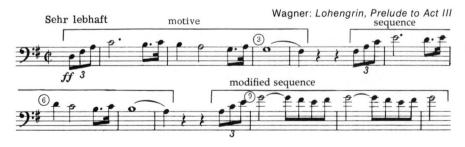

Sehr lebhaft   motive

Wagner: *Lohengrin, Prelude to Act III*
sequence

modified sequence

(d) Melodic, rhythmic, and harmonic sequences appear in this *Scarlatti variation*. The harmonic sequence consists of two chords (in brackets) in the left hand, and the melodic and rhythmic sequence is the descending three-note pattern in the right hand.

(e) A two-measure motive is repeated in a free sequence, followed by a new motive (measure 5) using the same rhythm in a descending pattern. This is also repeated in sequence. The same rhythmic pattern appears in measure 7.

(f) A scale-wise motive is repeated in sequence in contrary motion (inversion). When the notes ascend or descend in the motive, the corresponding notes in the sequence descend or ascend, respectively.

Bach: *Two-Part Invention No. 1*

(g) A two-measure motive outlining the tonic chord in C major is followed by a sequence outlining the V7 chord in contrary motion.

Haydn: *Symphony No. 94 ("Surprise"), Second Movement*

Motives may be developed and expanded in many ways. The preceding excerpts have indicated that unity in music may be achieved by an exact repetition or some sequential arrangement of the motive and that variety may be achieved by certain modifications of the motive melodically, harmonically, or rhythmically or by the use of new musical material. Structural balance, essential in music, is realized through the repetition (unity) and contrast of material (variety). This is the underlying principle in the form and structure of music.

ADDITIONAL EXAMPLES ILLUSTRATING THE USE OF THE MOTIVE

1. Humperdinck: Hansel and Gretel, "Evening Prayer."
2. Handel: The Messiah, "Behold the Lamb of God."
3. Rossini: The Barber of Seville, Overture.
4. Gounod: Faust, "Soldiers' Chorus."
5. Wagner: Tristan and Isolde, Prelude.
6. Beethoven: Symphony No. 7, Second Movement.
7. Mozart: Sonata for Piano K.189h, First Movement.
8. Schumann: Album for the Young, Op. 68 Nos. 1, 2, 38, 41.

The Phrase

We have seen that motives may be extended and expanded into various musical patterns and designs. Just as a book would be vague and difficult to read without sentence structure and an organized arrangement of words, so music would ramble aimlessly if musical patterns were not organized into shapes and contours. The basic unit of form that expresses a musical thought or idea is the *phrase*. A point of repose or rest in the music indicates the end of a phrase and is called a *cadence,* from the Latin word *cadere,* to fall. This refers to the falling inflection of the voice at the end of a sentence. The cadence is the most important factor in separating and determining these musical ideas, and it may create either a complete or a temporary break or pause in the music. The length of phrases may vary, but the four-measure phrase is the most common. The following three melodies illustrate phrases of varying lengths.

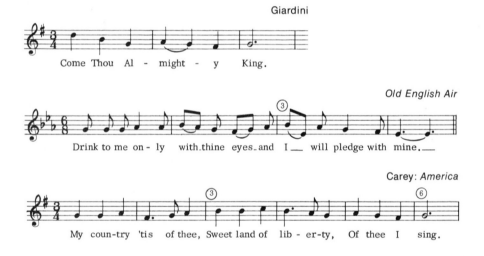

Giardini

Come Thou Al - might - y King.

Old English Air

Drink to me on - ly with thine eyes and I __ will pledge with mine. __

Carey: America

My coun-try 'tis of thee, Sweet land of lib - er-ty, Of thee I sing.

EXAMPLES OF PHRASES

1. The Schubert melody presents a complete musical thought and may be compared to the simple sentence in grammar. The four-measure phrase ends on the tonic chord (I) with its root (key tone) in the melody. This is a complete cadence and illustrates a perfect authentic cadence, authentic because it is a V to I cadence and perfect because it closes on the key tone in the melody.

Moderato   Schubert: *Wohin?*

2. A phrase is often the outgrowth and development of one or more melodic, harmonic, or rhythmic motives, either in repetition or in sequence. Here a four-measure phrase consists of a motive in measure 1, repeated in sequence in measure 2, and then followed by new material. The cadence closing the phrase is a semi- or half-cadence (V chord), a temporary point of rest. The musical thought is incomplete in this kind of cadence and another phrase or some kind of additional material is needed to complete the meaning.

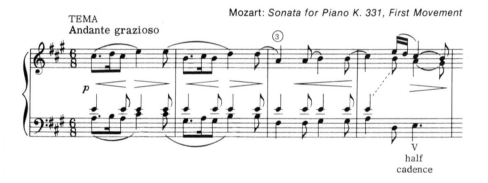

Mozart: *Sonata for Piano K. 331, First Movement*

TEMA
Andante grazioso

V
half
cadence

3. A phrase may end on the tonic chord (I) with the third (G) in the melody. This forms an incomplete cadence and becomes an imperfect authentic cadence (V-I) when the third (or fifth) of the tonic chord appears in the melody.

Andantino   *Irish Folk Song*

7

4. A cadence closing a phrase with the harmony of IV to I is a plagal cadence, sometimes referred to as the "Amen" cadence. Since this phrase ends with the root (key tone) of the tonic chord in the melody, it is a perfect plagal cadence.

5. A phrase may close on any tone or chord, at the discretion of the composer, but the previous examples are perhaps the most representative. Occasionally the IV chord substitutes for the V and forms a half-, or semi-, cadence.

6. This canon for three voices consists of three phrases, each four measures in length and each closing on the key tone of the key.

7. Most of the previous examples of the phrase have been four measures long. Phrases, however, may be extended by repetition of material, sequences, or a deceptive cadence. These are illustrated below.

(a) Schubert lengthens the phrase by the repetition of measures 3-4 an octave higher.

(b) He lengthens this phrase by the repetition of a two-measure motive in sequence.

(c) A phrase may be extended by a deceptive, or evaded, cadence.

This cadence (in measure 6) produces a feeling of incompleteness and surprise because of the use of a chord (VI) other than the tonic where a complete cadence is expected. An additional cadence is necessary to complete the phrase.

8. Frequently, a phrase that closes on a complete cadence is followed by an exact or modified repetition of the phrase. This is called a repeated phrase, which is illustrated in the following example.

Allegro moderato   Schubert: *Das Wandern*

SUMMARY

A phrase is the basic unit of musical form and may consist of either a complete or an incomplete musical thought. It is often developed by the use of a motive in repetition, sequence, or some other type of extension.

Cadences divide music into phrases. A complete cadence consists of a perfect authentic cadence (V or V₇ to I), or a perfect plagal cadence (IV to I) with the tonic or key tone in the melody. It corresponds to the period in grammar. An incomplete cadence consists of an imperfect authentic, an imperfect plagal, a half-, or semi-, cadence, or a deceptive cadence. The imperfect cadences end with either the third or fifth of the tonic chord in the melody. An incomplete cadence corresponds to the comma, semicolon, or question mark in grammar.

The Period

Two phrases join to form a *period* in music when the cadence of the first phrase is a half cadence or some other type of incomplete cadence and the second is complete. The first phrase is called the *antecedent* and the second the *consequent*.

1. The first phrase ends on a half cadence (measure 4) and the second on a complete cadence. Since the second phrase begins with the same melody as the first phrase, it is a parallel period.

Prokofiev: *Gavotte Op. 12, No. 2*

2. The first two phrases of the *Greensleeves* melody join to form a parallel period with a half cadence ending the first phrase and a complete cadence the second phrase.

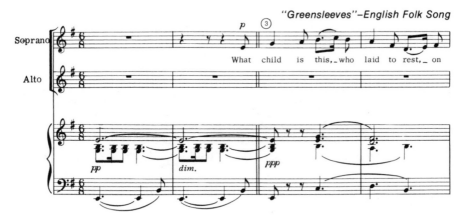

"Greensleeves"–English Folk Song

What child is this, who laid to rest, on

3. Another example of a parallel period is found in the first two phrases of this Irish folk song. The antecedent phrase closes on an incomplete cadence (tonic chord with the third in the melody) and the consequent phrase ends on a complete cadence. The melody of the second phrase begins the same as the first.

Irish Folk Song

4. The first two phrases of this Beethoven song form a period. The antecedent phrase ends on an incomplete cadence (the tonic with the third in the melody) in measure 4 and the second, or consequent, phrase closes on a complete cadence. Since the melodies in the two phrases are dissimilar, the period is called *contrasting*.

Beethoven: *Ich Liebe Dich (I Love Thee)*

Phrase repetitions often appear in the period form. When the repetition follows the original phrase consecutively, it does not alter the form but only extends it. Both the antecedent and consequent phrase are repeated in the French folk song.

French Folk Song

Only the consequent phrase is repeated in the following contrasting period.

Finnish Folk Song

SUMMARY

The period form consists of two phrases. The first, the antecedent phrase, closes on an incomplete cadence (a half cadence or imperfect cadence) and the second, the consequent phrase, closes on a complete cadence (usually authentic or plagal). The period is parallel when the second phrase begins the same as the first. If the second phrase is different, it is a contrasting period. While the cadences of the two phrases are different in a period form, they are the same in a repeated phrase; this is the chief distinction.

ADDITIONAL EXAMPLES OF THE PERIOD FORM

1. "Clementine", measures 1-8.
2. "Home on the Range", measures 1-8.

3. Schumann: *Album for the Young,* Op. 68, "The Wild Rider."
4. Nesmüller: *Der Tiroler und sein Kind,* measures 1-8.
5. Mozart: *Sonata for Piano in A Major* K.331, First Movement, measures 1-8.
6. Schubert: *Valse Nobles* Op. 77 No. 6, measures 1-8.
7. Haydn: *Symphony in G Major* ("Military"), Third Movement, measures 1-8.
8. Clementi: *Sonatina* Op. 36 No. 2, First Movement, measures 1-8.
9. Beethoven: *Sonata for Piano* Op. 10 No. 3, Third Movement, measures 1-16.
10. Bartok: *Mikrokosmos, Volume II, No. 62,* measures 1-12.
11. Prokofiev: *"Classical" Symphony* Op. 25, Second Movement, measures 5-20.

The Phrase Group

The *phrase group* usually consists of three phrases, the first two ending on incomplete cadences and the last one on a complete cadence. The phrase group serves as a substitute for the period form.

1. In the Brahms song, phrase 1 (repeated) and phrase 2 end on half cadences, and the last closes on a complete cadence.

Brahms: *Sandmänchen (The Little Sandman)*

2. The familiar carol *Silent Night* is an example of a phrase group. The first two phrases end on incomplete cadences.

Grüber: *Silent Night*

15

The theme of the second movement (variation) of Haydn's *String Quartet Op. 76 No. 3* is another example of the phrase-group. Here the phrase group is extended by the repetition of two of its phrases.

Haydn: *String Quartet Op. 76 No. 3, Second Movement*

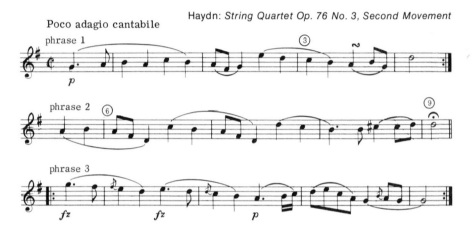

The Double Period

The *double period* contains four phrases: the first three ending on a half cadence or some other incomplete cadence and the final one closing on a complete cadence. The third phrase is usually either a repetition of the first phrase or is similar to it melodically and harmonically. The distinguishing feature of the double period is thăt the second phrase usually ends on a half cadence. This separates the form from two periods, or a repeated period. An immediate repetition of a phrase or period does not create a larger form; it merely extends and expands the original and basic form. Therefore, a repeated phrase is not a period and a repeated period is not a double period.

The following two examples illustrate the double period. The first phrase of each ends on an incomplete cadence, the second on a half cadence, the third on an incomplete cadence (same phrase as the first), and the last on a complete cadence.

Primary Units of Form

Russian *Folk Song*

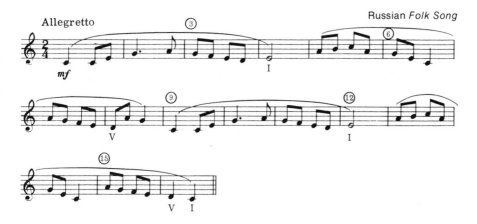

Moszkowski: *Spanish Dance Op. 12, No. 1*

EXAMPLES OF DOUBLE PERIOD

1. Beethoven: *Sonata for Piano* Op. 22, finale, measures 1-18.
2. Chopin: *Prelude* Op. 28 No. 10.
3. Mozart: *Sonata for Piano* K.205b, second movement, measures 1-17.
4. Schubert: *Grand Sonata for Piano in C Minor* No. 1, second movement, measures 1-14.
5. "Flow Gently, Sweet Afton."

CHAPTER 2

Part
Forms

Musical compositions consist of a series of recognizable divisions, or sections, and some combination of the smaller forms (phrase, period, phrase group, double period, and the like) into a larger unified whole. The underlying principle behind these forms and their development and evolution is the constant concern and need for a balance between unity and variety. The two-, three-, and five-part forms are the basic ones in shorter compositions and will be considered in this chapter.

The One-Part Form (A)

When a complete composition consists of only one of the primary units of form, such as phrase, period, phrase group, or double period, it is a *one-part form.*

1. This stanza of Brahms' song is a contrasting period and a

one-part form. The first phrase ends on a half cadence in measure 8. All of the stanzas of the poem are sung to the same music.

The Chopin *Prelude Op. 28 No. 1* is a one-part form, a parallel period. The first phrase closes on a half cadence (measure 8) and the second phrase is extended by sequence (to measure 25), followed by a short, concluding passage called a *codetta*.

Several of the examples of the primary units of form discussed in Chapter 1 are complete compositions and illustrate the one-part form. Refer to the following for review:

1. French folk song, page 14
2. Finnish folk song, page 14
3. *Silent Night*, page 15
4. *Sandmännchen*, Brahms—page 15
5. Russian folk song, page 17

The Binary or Two-Part Form (AB)

The two-part form (AB) is the smallest of the combined units of form and is composed of two sections or divisions, each ending on a complete cadence. Each part is contrasting in material and there is no return to the original idea (first part), although the two parts may end similarly and a motive may at times be common to both parts. Part I (or A) may end in the tonic key or it may modulate to the dominant or some other key. The two-part form, which was quite popular in the Baroque period, served as the basis for much of the instrumental music of Bach, Couperin, Rameau, and Scarlatti.

EXAMPLES OF THE TWO-PART FORM

1. This Slovak folk song is a two-part form with each part a repeated phrase. Notice that each ends on the key tone, for a complete cadence.

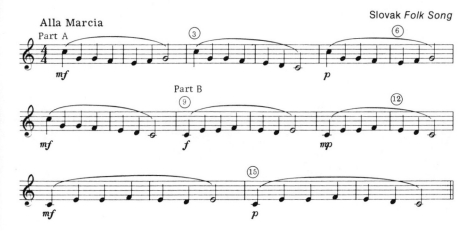

2. Part A—a parallel period (measures 1-8).
   Part B—a repeated phrase.
   Notice that the last two measures of each part are identical.

Presto   Swedish *Folk Song*

3. Part A—contrasting period (measures 1-8).
   Part B—parallel period (measure 9 to end).

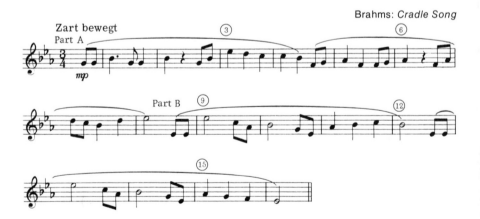

Zart bewegt   Brahms: *Cradle Song*

4. Part A—a repeated phrase (measures 1-8).

Part B—a repeated period (measures 9-16 and measure 17 to the end).

Bartok: *Six Miniatures, No. 1*

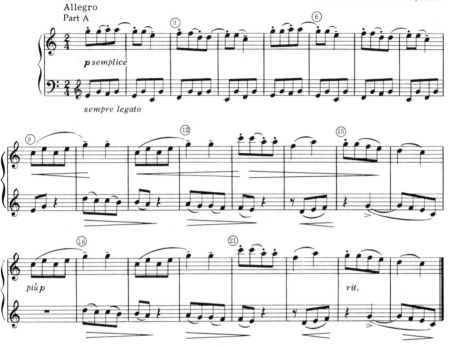

5. Part A—a contrasting period (measures 1-8), modulating to the dominant key.

Part B—a contrasting period (measure 9 to the end), returning to the tonic key. The last four measures are an extension.

Mozart, *To Friendship*

The term *barform* is often used to designate the pattern AAB. It is based on old German poetry, in which there were two similar stanzas (AA) and a contrasting closing one (B). Wagner uses this form frequently in *Die Meistersinger*.

ADDITIONAL EXAMPLES OF THE TWO-PART FORM

1. Bach, selections from *Anna Magdalena's Notebook*.
   (a) Aria
   (b) Polonaise (note similar cadence in both parts)
   (c) March
   (d) Minuet
       Part A—period
       Part B—repeated period

2. Brahms, *Waltzes Op. 39* Nos. 3, 8, 9, and 10

3. Handel, Theme from *Air With Variations* ("The Harmonious Blacksmith")

4. Schumann, *Chorale* from *Album for the Young, Op. 68* No. 4
   Part A—a repeated period (measures 1-8)
   Part B—a double period (measures 9 to the end)

5. Mozart, *Minuet* from *Don Giovanni*
   Each part is a period

6. Bartok, *Mikrokosmos, Volume I, No. 31*

7. Haydn, *Symphony No. 73 in D (La Chasse)*, Third Movement, Trio

8. Prokofiev, *Symphony Op. 25 (Classical)*, Third Movement (measures 1-12)

9. Mozart, *String Quartet in E♭ K428*, Third Movement, Trio

10. Beethoven, *Feuerfarb*

The Ternary or Three-Part Form (ABA)

The two-part form combines two contrasting sections in a unified structure. However, the need and desire for repetition through a return of all or a portion of Part A was met by the three-part form. The basic plan is statement, new material, and re-statement. Its salient feature is the return of the beginning statement, which offers unity and balance to the music. Variety and contrast are achieved by the introduction of new material. The ternary is the most frequently found form in music and extends from the simplest folk song melody to highly sophisticated symphonic works. The term, arch form, is frequently used to designate ABA. It is based on the idea of an arch which connects the initial and final statements of the principal theme.

EXAMPLES OF THE THREE-PART FORM (ABA)

1. The simplest example of the three-part form is illustrated in this German folk song. Each part is only a phrase of four measures.

2. Part A consists of a repeated phrase.
   Part B is a phrase ending on the dominant chord (half cadence).
   Part A is a phrase.

3. This "Theme" from Beethoven's *Twelve Variations* illustrates the most frequently found three-part form in smaller works. Here Part A is a period, Part B is a phrase, and Part A returns and repeats

the consequent phrase of the original period. Notice that Part B is an outgrowth and variation of Part A.

Allegretto   Beethoven: *Twelve Variations, Theme*

This type of ternary form is sometimes called a rounded binary form (A/B) or an incipient ternary form when the B section ends on an incomplete cadence (usually the dominant) followed by a return of part of the A section. See also Example 2 (Dutch folk song) on page 26.

4. A more detailed analysis of the organization of the following *Song Without Words Op. 30 No. 6* of Mendelssohn is given below.

Introduction (measures 1-6)

These measures establish the accompaniment pattern and set the mood for the piece through the use of the tonic chord. A two-note figure (E♯ and G♯) appears in the right hand in measures 3-4. This figure reappears several times in the body of the piece as a unifying influence, or "basic motive."

Part A (measures 7-21)

This is a parallel period with a half cadence in measures 13-14. Notice the two-note motive from the introduction.

Part B (measures 23-30)

This part consists of a phrase extended by sequence ending on the dominant chord. Again, the two-note figure is heard (measure 29).

Interlude (measures 31-36)

In measures 31-32 the accompaniment repeats the last two measures of the introduction as preparation for the return of Part A. However, this return is delayed by an extension or interlude of four measures, which lead into Part A.

Part A (measures 37-43)

Only the consequent phrase of the parallel period of Part A returns.

Repetition of *Parts B* and *A*

In the score, repeat marks in measure 42 indicate the repeat of Parts B and A. This extends the form but is not essential and does not change the basic plan of the three-part form.

Codetta (measure 44 to the end)

This is a short concluding passage which extends the piece and emphasizes the dominant and tonic harmony.

Mendelssohn: *Song Without Words Op. 30 No. 6*

Basic Forms in Music

5. Tschaikowsky, *Dance of the Swans* from *Swan Lake.*
   Introduction—one measure.
   Part A—a repeated phrase (measures 2-9).
   Part B—a double period (measures 10-25).
   Part A returns (measure 26), followed by a short codetta
measure 34).

Tschaikowsky: *Swan Lake, Dance of the Swans*

Part Forms

ADDITIONAL EXAMPLES OF THREE-PART FORM

1. Schumann, *Album for the Young, Op. 68*
   No. 1—*Melody*
   No. 2—*Soldier's March*
   No. 3—*Humming Song*
   No. 5—*A Little Piece*
   No. 6—*The Poor Orphan*
   No. 8—*The Wild Rider*
   No. 9—*Folk Song*
   > Part A—parallel period
   > Part B—two two-measure phrases (repeated)
   > Part A—parallel period

2. Chopin, *Preludes, Op. 28*
   No. 13
   No. 21
   > Part A—contrasting period
   > Part B—repeated phrase
   > Part A—extended phrase altered

3. Debussy, *Preludes, Book I*
   No. 3
   > Introduction
   > Part A
   > Introduction as interlude
   > Part A (repeated)
   > Part B
   > Introduction as interlude
   > Part A (transposed)
   > Part A in original key

4. Stravinsky, *Berceuse* from *The Firebird*
   Part A—a repeated phrase (listen for the ostinato in the harp and viola parts).
   Part B—repeated phrase
   Part A returns, followed by codetta

5. Praetorius, *Lo, How a Rose E'er Blooming*
   A. repeated phrase
   B. phrase (two measures)
   A. phrase

6. Mendelssohn, *Songs Without Words*
   Op. 67 No. 5
   Op. 58, No. 2
   Op. 102, No. 3
      Long extension of Part B and coda
7. Copland, *Four Piano Blues*, No. 3
8. Bartok, *Mikrokosmos*, Vol. I, No. 24
9. Debussy, *The Little Shepherd* from *The Children's Corner*

The Five-Part Form (ABACA)*

The five-part form (ABACA) is an outgrowth and extension of the three-part form, with the addition of another section, or part, followed by a return to Part A. It is similar to the three-part form where Parts B and A are repeated (ABABA), except that the repeated B (fourth section) is replaced by a section differing in pitch, or materials. This new section may be completely new material, a somewhat altered version of Part B (sometimes using the same or similar motive from another section), or an exact or modified transposition of Part B.

Schumann's *Nachtstück* is an example of the five-part form. Its outline is:

Introduction (measures 1-2).
Part A—parallel period (measures 3-10).
Part B—phrase (measures 11-14).
Part A—parallel period (measures 15-22).
Part C—repeated phrase (measures 23-33) employing a similar motive from Part B. The last two chords repeat the chords of the Introduction.
Part A—parallel period (measures 34-41). The second phrase is slightly altered.
Codetta (measures 41 on).

---

* Since the rondo form (see Chapter 3) is defined as a primary or principal theme alternating with one or more secondary themes, the five-part form (ABACA) is sometimes called a "five-part rondo."

Basic Forms in Music

Part C
Più mosso

Part A
Primo Tempo

Codetta

ADDITIONAL EXAMPLES OF THE FIVE-PART FORM

Mendelssohn, *Song Without Words Op. 67 No. 4 ("Spinning Song")*.
Introduction—two measures.
Part A—parallel period (measures 3-10).

Mendelssohn, *Song Without Words,*
Op. 67, No. 4 ("Spinning Song")

Part B—phrase extended by sequence (measures 11-25).

Transition (measures 25-29).
Part A (measures 30-41).
Part B (transposed) (measures 42-56).
Transition (measures 56-64).
Part A (measures 65-80).
Codetta (measures 80 on).

2. Beethoven, *Sonata for Piano, Op. 13 ("Pathetique")*.
Second Movement
Part A—contrasting period repeated (measures 1-16).

Beethoven, *Sonata,*
Op. 13 ("Pathetique"), Second Movement

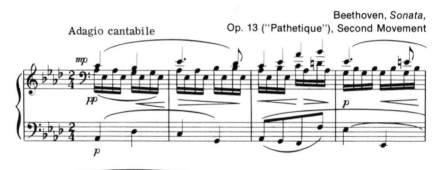

Part B—phrase extended (measures 17-28).

Part A—a period (measures 29-36).

Part C—a parallel period based on a two-measure motive (measures 37-41).

Transition based upon a motive of Part C (measures 45-50).

Part A—repeated period (measures 51-66).

Codetta (measures 67 on).

3. An irregular five-part form is illustrated in the *Mazurka Op. 7 No. 3* of Chopin where the form is ABCDA. Unity is achieved by the immediate repetition of each part and the return of Part A at the end.

Introduction

Part A

Chopin: *Mazurka Op. 7 No. 3.*

Part B

Part C

Part D

The introduction appears as an interlude.
Part A returns.
Short codetta.

4. Prokofiev, *March* from *The Love of Three Oranges*

5. Chopin, *Mazurkas Op. 6 No. 1; Op. 6 No. 2* and *Op. 6 No. 3* (ABCDA); *Op. 30 No. 2* (ABCB with codetta)

6. Chopin, *Prelude Op. 28*
   No. 17
         A—period extended
         B—period (or two phrases)
         A—antecedent phrase only
         C—phrase group extended at cadence
         A—modified repetition

7. Mozart, *Recodare* from *Requiem Mass*

CHAPTER 3

The Rondo Form

The word *rondo* is derived from the French word, *rondeau,* which is a poem in which the opening and closing lines are identical. The musical rondo form is based on this principle of repetition of material and can be traced to the early folk songs and tunes in which a refrain or chorus is repeated after each verse. Its characteristic design and plan is the return of the principal or primary theme, alternating with secondary themes and sections. The five-part form (discussed in Chapter 2) is of the rondo family, with the principal theme returning twice. There are two general types of rondos, the old rondeau or rondino (simple type) of the seventeenth and eighteenth centuries, and the classical rondo of the late eighteenth and nineteen centuries.

Rondeau (Simple Rondo)

In the simple rondo each section consists of a one-part form, usually a period or its equivalent. It was popular in the instrumental music of the seventeenth century and was used extensively by Rameau, Scarlatti, Handel, and Bach.

1. *Les Tourbillons (The Whirlwind)*, Dandrieu
    The overall form of this composition is ABACA.
    Part A—a repeated period
    Part B—a group of phrases
    Part A—a repeated period
    Part C—a period with each phrase extended by sequence
    Part A—a repeated period

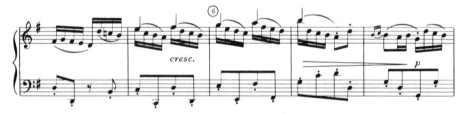

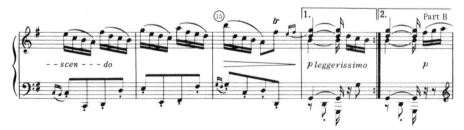

2. Krenek, *Rondo* from *Eight Piano Pieces*

Krenek employs the old simple rondo form (ABACABA) in this short composition, which uses the 12-tone technique:

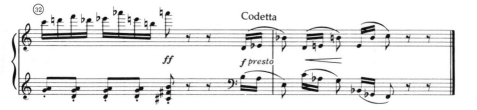

ADDITIONAL EXAMPLES OF THE SIMPLE RONDO

1. Rameau, *Les Tourbillons.*
   Part A—contrasting period (consequent phrase is extended).
   Part B—phrase group (third phrase extended by sequence).
   Part A—identical to original Part A.
   Part C—phrase group (second phrase extended).
   Part A—same as before.

2. Couperin, *Pieces de Clavecin, La Bandoline.*
   The form is ABACADA. Note the similarity of the parts.
3. Rameau, *Musette en Rondeau.*

The Classical Rondo

With the growth of instrumental music in the eighteenth century, the rondo form progressed from the simple part-form type to a more complex form called the *classical rondo,* in which one or more of its sections was lengthened and extended to a two- or three-part form. The result is a compound form which is the chief distinction between the old rondeau and the classical rondo. Most often, Part A is the compound form. If Part A returns once, it is a first rondo; if it returns twice, it is a second rondo; and three times, a third rondo. Naturally, the classical rondo is usually more extended than the preclassic form and has a more involved structure. Frequently there are transitions, or "bridge material," which connect the various sections and extend the composition.

FIRST RONDO

Beethoven, *Piano Sonata Op. 2 No. 1,* Second Movement.

This movement falls into the first rondo classification because Part A is a three-part form in itself and returns once.

Part A—a three-part form (aba). (Notice the use of small letters for the subdivisions within a part.)

(a) parallel period.

(b) phrase.

(a) parallel period.

Part B—period (the second phrase modulates to C major and is extended).

Part A—three-part form (aba). The themes are embellished and varied.

Codetta

Beethoven: *Piano Sonata Op. 2 No. 1, Second Movement*

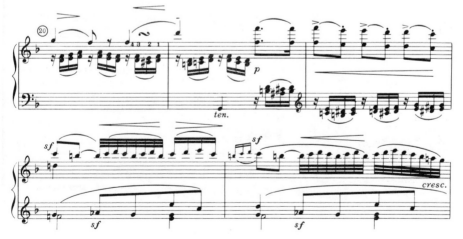

ADDITIONAL EXAMPLES OF THE FIRST RONDO FORM

    1. Beethoven, *Violin Sonata, Op. 12 No. 3,* Second Movement.
        Part A—three-part form.
            (a) parallel period (repeated).
            (b) phrase (these four measures are similar to a short transition).

            (a) consequent phrase of the original period only.
        Part B—period (includes two versions of the antecedent phrase).
        Part A—only "a" (parallel period) returns.
        Coda—last 26 measures.
    2. Schumann, *Symphony No. 1 in B♭ Major,* Second Movement.
        Part A—a three-part form (aba); the return of "a" is transposed.
        Part B—an extended phrase (sequence).
        Part A—reduced to "a" only.

3. Mendelssohn, *Notturno* from *A Midsummer Night's Dream.*
Part A—three-part form (aba)
    (a) period.
    (b) two phrases.
    (a) reduced to consequent phrase of original "a".
Part B—phrase group.
Part A—reduced to one part (the "a" of the original Part A).
Coda—in two sections.

4. An interesting variant of the first rondo form is found in the last movement of the Mozart *Piano Sonata, K.331 (Turkish March).* Each of the parts (aba) is followed by a refrain.

SECOND RONDO

The second rondo consists of a composition in which there are two returns of the principal theme, or section, and in which one of the sections is a two- or three-part form. The second movement, "Romanze," from Mozart, *Eine Kleine Nachtmusik, K.525,* is an illustration of this form.

Part A—a three-part form (aba):
    (a) parallel period (measures 1-8):
    (b) two similar phrases (measures 8-16):
    (a) reduced to the consequent phrase of the original period (measures 13-16):
    Part B—two similar phrases and transition (measures 17-30)
    Part A—only one part (the "a" of the original Part A) (measures 31-38)
    Part C—two phrases employing a three-note motive in imitation (measures 38-50)
    Part A—a three-part form as before (measures 50-66)
    Codetta—motive from "a" of Part A (measures 66 on)

Mozart: *Eine Kleine Nachtmusik K.525, Romanze*

Part C

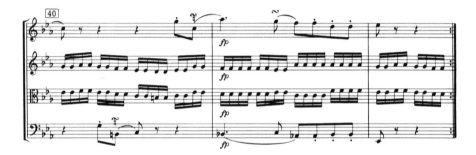

ADDITIONAL EXAMPLES OF THE SECOND RONDO

1. Beethoven, *Piano Sonata Op. 49 No. 2*, Second Movement.
   Part A—three-part form (aba) (measures 1-20):
      (a) parallel period
      (b) phrase
      (a) parallel period

Beethoven: *Piano Sonata Op. 49 No. 2, Second Movement*

Transition modulating to the dominant key (D) (measures 21-27)

Part B—parallel period (measures 28-36):

Extension of cadence and transition (measures 36-47).
Part A—same as original (measures 48-67).
Part C—three-part (aba) (measures 68-79).

    (a) phrase
    (b) phrase
    (a) phrase

Transition using motive of "b" of Part C (measures 80-87)
Part A—three-part form as before (measures 88-107).
Codetta—motive from "a" of Part A (measure 108 on).
2. Mozart, *Rondo in A Minor K.511.*

All of the parts are three-part forms which extend the composition considerably. Notice repetitions, transitions, evaded cadence, the shortened return of the principal part, and the use of a melodic figure.
3. Beethoven, *Für Elise.*
A concise example of the second rondo form.
4. Brahms, *Symphony No. 1,* Third Movement.
5. Schubert, *Piano Sonato in D Major Op. 53,* Last Movement.
The form is extended considerably.
6. Bartok, *Three Rondos, No. 1.*

Third Rondo

In this form, Part A returns three times, and one or more parts is a two- or three-part form.
1. Beethoven, *Piano Sonata in C Major Op. 2 No. 3,* Last Movement.
The basic plan and outline of the movement is:

Part A—aba
Part B—a
Part A—a
Part C—aba
Part A—aba
Part B—repeated in tonic key
Coda—the first theme (a) of Part A appears in coda.

It is common for the first part ["a"] of the Part A to appear in the coda as the last statement.

Beethoven: *Piano Sonata
in C Major Op. 2 No. 3, Last Movement*

Part A

Part C

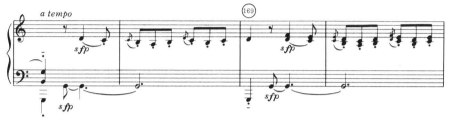

Part A

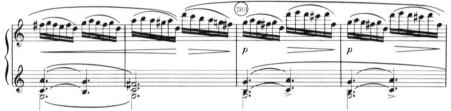

Part B

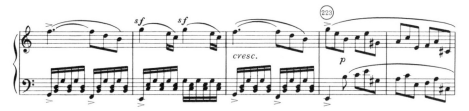

Coda
a) of Part A

SUMMARY

The most obvious feature of the rondo form is the recurring principal theme. The old rondino, or rondeau, consists of a principal theme that alternates with secondary themes, each a one-part form in itself.

The classical rondo is a compound form in which one or more of its sections or parts is a two- or three-part form. Part A is the principal one; when it repeats once, it is a first rondo; when it appears twice, it is a second rondo; and three times, a third rondo.

ADDITIONAL EXAMPLES OF THE THIRD RONDO FORM

1. Beethoven, *Piano Sonatas Op. 2 No. 2 in A Major* and *Op. 13 in C Minor,* Last Movement of each.
2. Brahms, *Violin and Piano Sonata No. 2 in A Major Op. 100,* Last Movement.
3. Beethoven, *Symphony No. 6 in F Major Op. 68 (Pastorale),* Finale.

The last statement of the principal theme merges with the coda.

CHAPTER 4

Song
Form
and
Trio

Another extension and expansion of the basic ternary design and a combination of two forms is the *song form and trio*. It originated in eighteenth-century dances, in which the second dance in a series was called the trio and used only three instruments. The three horns used in the trio of Beethoven's Third Symphony is an example of this practice.

The song form is the principal section or division of this type of structure and is sometimes called the *principal song*. It is a complete part form in itself, usually AB or ABA. The term "song" indicates that the parts or divisions of the form are small enough to be identified with the song. The trio (subordinate song) that follows is usually contrasting in character, style, and often in key. No doubt based on an earlier idea of offering contrasting music for each couple's turn in the dance, these two sections give the aural impression of two separate, short compositions. The first section (song form) then returns either in exact duplication (usually a da capo repeat, meaning from the "head" or beginning), or in some modified form. A balance is therefore maintained between unity by repetition and contrast by new material. Seldom is there a transition into the trio, but frequently a transitional passage closes the trio leading into the return of the song form, or principal song. Although any type of composition or movement may follow this form, it is most often found in marches and in the third movement of sonatas, symphonies, string quartets, etc., where it bears the specific names, Minuetto and Trio or Scherzo and Trio.

Even though there are a number of variants and distinctive characteristics of the form, the general outline is this:

song form (principal song)   trio   song form (da capo repeat)
    ABA   ABA   ABA

The Second movement, Minuetto and Trio, of Mozart's *Viennese Sonatina No. 2* offers a clear, concise example of the song form and trio design. The minuetto is the song form section and is a three-part form:

Part A (measures 1-8).
Part B (measures 9-12).
Part A (measures 13-20).

The Trio is also a three-part form:

Part A (measures 21-28).
Part B (measures 29-32).
Part A (measures 33 to end of trio).

The repetition of the minuetto (song form) in a da capo repeat completes the three divisions of the form.

Mozart: *Viennese Sonatina No. 2,*
Minuetto and Trio

In the Minuetto and Trio Movement (Third) of the Haydn *String Quartet in D Minor Op. 76 No. 2,* both sections are three-part (ABA) forms. Notice the canonic imitation in the Minuetto.

Haydn: *String Quartet in D Minor Op. 76 No. 2,*
Menuetto and Trio

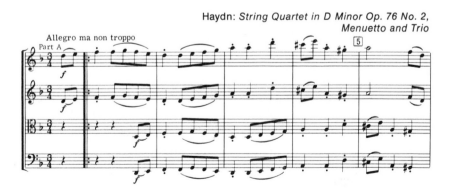

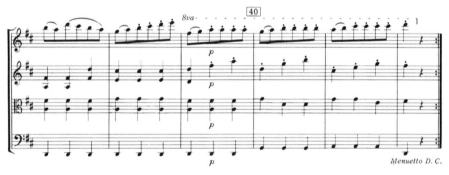

Prokofiev labels the third movement of his "Classical" Symphony Op. 25, *Gavotte* and *Trio.* This movement follows the song form and trio design. (The Gavotte is in binary form [AB].)

Gavotte (AB).

A—phrase (measures 1-4).

B—contrasting period (measures 5-12).

Trio (A).

A—a repeated period.

Gavotte—an exact repetition of the original section.

Song Form and Trio

Prokofiev: *"Classical" Symphony Op. 25,*
Gavotte and Trio

The principle of repetition may be emphasized and the composition expanded and extended by the return of the trio section in either an exact or a modified manner. The third movement of Beethoven's *Fourth Symphony* is illustrative of this kind of extension. The general plan is:

Song Form (ABA).
Trio (ABA).
Song Form—an exact statement of the original
Trio—an exact repetition of the original Trio.
Song Form—this section consists of a brief return to the original song form, followed by a codetta.

Somewhat parallel to the principle of the five-part form is the song form with two different trios. An example of this form is the Third Movement of Dvorak's *Symphony in E Minor ("From the New World")*. A brief outline is given for this movement (scherzo and trio) in "Additional Examples."

One of the most frequent uses of the song form and trio is found in marches. Often the return to the song form (da capo) is omitted. Sousa's *Stars and Stripes Forever* illustrates this shortened version. The song form is binary and the trio is ternary.

SUMMARY

The design of the song form and trio consists of three divisions, or sections, and is usually heard as two separate compositions, with the first one repeated after the second. Each of the three sections is usually a two- or three-part form. Occasionally the trio is only one part, and the return to the song form may be shortened or in some way modified. Any type of composition may follow the plan of this form, but its most frequent appearance is in marches (often no return to the first section after the trio) and in the third movements of sonatas, symphonies, string quartets, etc. The form may be extended and lengthened by an exact or modified repetition of the trio after the repetition of the song form or by the addition of a second trio.

ADDITIONAL EXAMPLES OF THE SONG FORM AND TRIO

1. Dvorak, *Symphony in E Minor ("From the New World")*, Third Movement.

    Song form (Scherzo). Ternary (ABA)
        Introduction (measures 1-12).
        Part A—repeated phrase (measures 13-29).
        Part B—extended phrase (measures 29-40).
        Part A—repeated phrase (measures 41-59).
    Transition (measures 60-67).
    Trio I—Ternary (ABA).
        Part A—repeated period (measures 68-83).
        Part B—repeated phrase (measures 84-91).
        Part A—period (measures 92-98).
    Transition and extension (measures 99-122).
    Song form (scherzo) reduced to the repeat of Part A in original song form (measures 123-141).

Transition (measures 142-175).

Trio II—Ternary (ABA).

Part A—repeated period (measures 176-191).

Part B—repeated period extended (measures 192-222).

Part A—repeated period (measures 223-238).

Transition (measures 239-247).

Scherzo—three-part form as originally stated (measures 248-302).

Extension and transition (measures 303-314).

Trio I is repeated (measures 315-345).

Transition (measures 346-369).

Scherzo is reduced to second A of the first scherzo (measures 370-388).

Coda (measure 389 on).

2. Chopin, *Waltz in E minor (Posthumous)*.
Introduction.
Song form (ABA).
Trio (ABA).
Song form (only Part A of the original song form returns).

3. Chopin, *Mazurka, Op. 7 No. 2*.
Song form (ABA).
Trio (ABA).
Song form (ABA).

4. Schumann, *Album for the Young Op. 68 No. 11*.

5. Smetana, *String Quartet, Polka*.

6. Tschaikowsky, *Nutcracker Suite, March*.
Trio is a one-part form.

7. Ravel, *Le Tombeau de Couperin, Minuet*.

8. Debussy, *The Children's Corner, Golliwog's Cake Walk*.

9. Chopin, *Prelude D♭ Major Op. 28 No. 15*.

10. Schubert, *March Militaire*. Each section is three parts.

11. Examples with Two Trios.

Schumann, *Symphony No. 1 in B♭, Op. 68 (Spring)*, Third Movement.

Brahms, *Symphony No. 2 in D Major, Op. 73*, Third Movement.

12. Chopin, *Mazurkas*.
Op. 17 No. 1—Trio is one-part.
Op. 59 No. 3—Da Capo reduced to one part.

13. Boccherini, *Minuet Op. 7 No. 3*.
Song Form.

      A (repeated period).
      B (phrase).
      A (period).
   Trio (subdominant key).
      A—period.
      B—repeated phrase.
      A—period.

14. The third movements of Haydn and Mozart Symphonies.
15. Tschaikowsky, *March* from *Nutcracker Suite.*
    The return of the song form is a literal one.
16. Beethoven, *Symphony No. 8*, Third Movement.
17. Mendelssohn, *Symphony No. 4 (Italian)*, Third Movement.
18. Bizet, *Micaela's Aria* from *Carmen.*
    Trio begins with the change in tempo from andante to allegro.
19. Ravel, *String Quartet*, Second Movement.

CHAPTER 5

Variation Forms

Probably the oldest and most prevalent device in musical composition is that of variation. Generally speaking, any modified or varied repetition of a musical element falls in this category. Its fundamental premise is based on the idea of presenting a musical idea in a number of alterations and modifications. The variation may be melodic, harmonic, or rhythmic, and it may be applied to the bass line, melodic line, harmony, or rhythm. Its influence is felt in all kinds of music of all periods, and the composer's skill in the use of variation has received the highest respect and esteem from the Middle Ages to the present time. Variation ranges from the simplest change or embellishment in a melody, chord pattern, or rhythm to a highly sophisticated composition in which the variations are subtle, complex, and free in structure.

Variation in music appears as a device and as a form. Any one of the elements of music—rhythm, melody, or harmony—may be altered and varied in some way. Here it serves as a compositional device. It may also appear as the principal design or form itself, in which the total structure consists of variants of some musical material.

Various examples of the variation principle will be illustrated in the following compositions.

Ground Bass and Bass Ostinato*

Of all the variation types possibly the easiest to recognize and hear is the ground bass, or bass ostinato. A short melodic motive is repeated over and over in the bass part as a fixed framework, with new and free material appearing melodically and harmonically in the upper parts. This recurring bass is a unifying influence in the music and serves as a challenge for variety and innovation in the melody and harmony. Its organization is similar to the contemporary idea of the boogie-woogie bass. Composers of all periods have used the ground bass and ostinato as a compositional device, at times throughout a complete composition and as a device within certain sections of a composition.

An early example of the ostinato is found in the thirteenth-century English madrigal, *Sumer is icumen in.* The melody is organized as a canon. The bass part has its own individual phrase, which is repeated throughout the canon and serves as an ostinato bass.

*The ground bass is sometimes defined as a motive consisting of only one or two measures, while the bass ostinato is somewhat longer. For our purposes, the two terms will be considered as synonymous.

A famous seventeenth-century example of the bass ostinato is the *Lament* from the opera, *Dido and Aeneas* by Henry Purcell. A five-measure phrase consisting of a descending chromatic scale is introduced alone in the bass and repeated six times, with contrasting material above it. The bass tones are used as chord tones for the harmonic structure of the music; suspensions and other nonharmonic tones add variety and horizontal movement to the music.

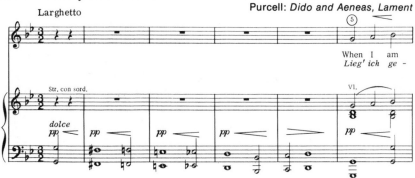

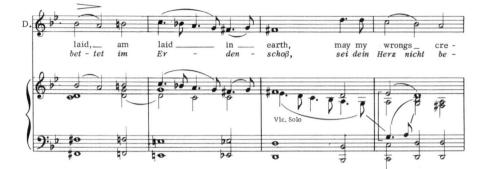

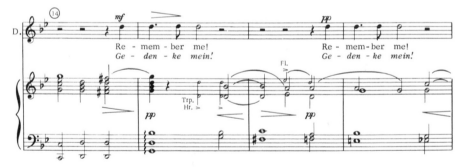

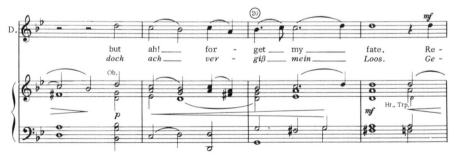

mem-ber me, but ah____ for - get____ my fate!
den - ke mein, doch ach____ ver - giß____ mein Los!

An eighteenth-century example of the ostinato is the *Crucifixus* from Bach's *Mass in B Minor.* The ostinato is quite similar to the Purcell example, with its chromatic stepwise movement. It is repeated 12 times and presented initially in a harmonic setting. The voice part is quite contrapuntal in texture. Notice the use of short motives in imitation.

Bach: *Mass in B Minor, Crucifixus*

A number of composers have employed the ostinato as a device for a relatively short time within a section of a composition. For example, an ostinato bass of four notes introduces the subordinate theme in the last movement of the Brahms *Symphony No. 1 in C Minor:*

Brahms: *Symphony No. 1 in C Minor, Fourth Movement*

In the last movement of the Tschaikowsky *Symphony No. 5,* an ostinato bass accompanies the return of the theme in the recapitulation. After eight measures, the parts are reversed and the ostinato appears above the theme.

Tschaikowsky: *Symphony No. 5, Last Movement*

Parts are reversed (double counterpoint).

In the *Procession of the Knights* in Act I of *Parsifal,* Wagner repeats a basic motive in the bass:

Wagner: *Parsifal, Act I, Procession of the Knights*

The Hymn of Jesus by Gustav Holst opens with a bass ostinato which becomes a characteristic device throughout the composition:

Holst: *The Hymn of Jesus*

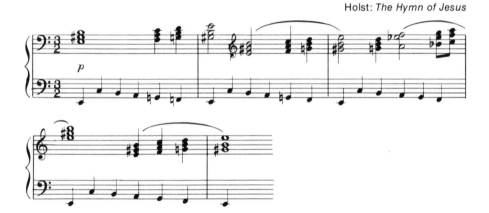

As mentioned earlier, one of the contemporary equivalents of this kind of persistent bass line is the boogie-woogie device. A short example illustrates this style:

"The Sloop John B."

ADDITIONAL EXAMPLES OF THE BASS OSTINATO

1. Henry Cowell, *Three Ostinati with Chorales for Clarinet and Piano.*
2. Roy Harris, *Andante Ostinato Op. 1.*
3. Brahms, *Variations on a Theme by Haydn* (Finale).

4. Darius Milhaud, *Sumare* from *Saudades do Brazil.*
5. Arensky, *Bass Ostinato.*
6. Sibelius, from the *Land of a Thousand Lakes (Sibeliana), Pastorale.*
7. Honneger, from *King David, Cortege.*
8. Stravinsky, *Symphony of Psalms.*
9. Sibelius, *Symphony No. 2 in D Major* (Finale).
   The last movement begins with a two-note ostinato in the violas
and cellos.

Another ostinato bass accompanies the subordinate theme in the same movement.

10. In the *Interludium* from Hindemith's *Ludus Tonalis*, a one-measure motive is repeated six times in the bass in the first section of the composition (measures 1-9):

The motive is then transposed, followed by a new ostinato (measure 15), and the original motive returns in measure 19. After a short middle section (10 measures), the first section is repeated a whole step lower.

Passacaglia

Another type of variation is the *passacaglia*, which also has a repeated bass line. It is derived from an old Spanish dance in triple meter. In most instances composers have made little distinction between the ostinato and the passacaglia and have used the two terms interchangeably. Since the Bach *Passacaglia in C Minor* for organ is regarded as the outstanding example of this form and represents the model and standard of the design, its features and characteristics will serve as the basis for our discussion of the passacaglia.

Bach, *Organ Passacaglia and Fugue in C Minor.*

The theme, or ostinato, is a phrase of eight measures, in triple meter and in a minor key. It is longer than many of the bass ostinatos and is stated alone at the beginning, followed by 20 variations. Even though the composition is a continuous whole in its organization, it is convenient to consider the repetitions as "variations." A triple fugue with the bass line as the subject follows the passacaglia.

Passacaglia theme: Bach: *Organ Passacaglia and Fugue in C Minor*

Variation I and II—A harmonic treatment with this motive:

Variation III—Three-voiced counterpoint in eighth notes

Variation IV—Contrapuntal with this rhythmic figure

Variation V—The bass ostinato is modified

etc.

This figure becomes the basis for the imitative contrapuntal texture of the upper part.

Variations VI, VII, and VIII

The texture of the sixteenth-note movement increases from one voice to two and three voices in the three variations. The ostinato appears in its original rhythm.

Variation IX—The ostinato is varied rhythmically

The same rhythmic pattern appears in the upper voices.

Variation X—Scale passages and chords accompany the ostinato

Variation XI—Scale passages continue with the ostinato transferred to the top voice

Variation XII—Ostinato in top voice accompanied by imitative motives in eighth and sixteenth notes, respectively

Variation XIII—Ostinato in inner voice modified melodically and rhythmically

Variation XIV—Ostinato appears in the first note of a group of sixteenth notes in arpeggio form in the left hand

Variation XV—Ostinato returns to the bass line

Variation XVI—Triplet accompaniment to ostinato

Variation XVII—A slight change in rhythm in the ostinato

etc.

Accompanying counterpoint uses the rhythmic pattern of Variation IV.

Variation XVIII—Ostinato returns to original design with a more active rhythmic pattern

Variation XIX—Short motives are repeated above the basic ostinato and form their own ostinato

etc.

This part appears in the right hand. The left hand reverses the voices.

The second song, *Die Darstellung Mariä im Tempel,* from *Das Marienleben* by Hindemith is a passacaglia. The seven-measure phrase appears in the accompaniment as an ostinato and is repeated in a series of variations (17).

Hindemith: *Das Marienleben,*
Die Darstellung Mariä in Tempel

Some alterations of the motive are illustrated in the following examples. The first two measures of each are given.

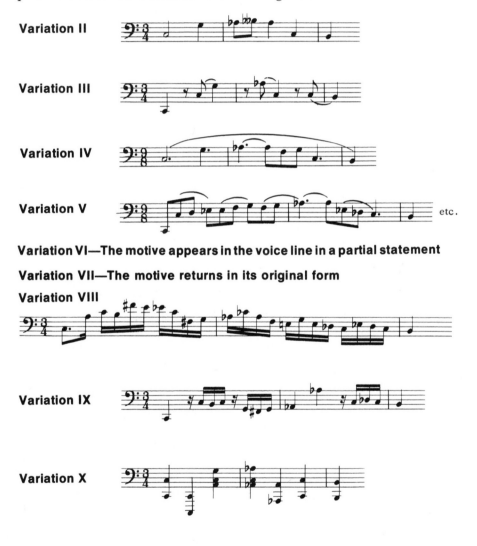

Variation II

Variation III

Variation IV

Variation V

etc.

Variation VI—The motive appears in the voice line in a partial statement

Variation VII—The motive returns in its original form

Variation VIII

Variation IX

Variation X

Variation XI

Variation XII

Variation XIII

Variation XIV

The *passacaglia* from the opera *Peter Grimes* by Benjamin Britten opens with this motive in the cellos and basses. The motive begins on a different beat of the measure in each repetition:

Britten: *Peter Grimes, Passacaglia*

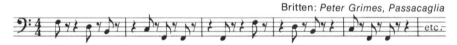

ADDITIONAL EXAMPLES OF THE PASSACAGLIA

1. Hindemith, *String Quartet No. 4*, Last Movement.
   The phrase is heard in the cello at the beginning:

Hindemith: *String Quartet No. 4, Last Movement*

Listen for changes in register, altered rhythms, canonic imitation, melodic alterations, use of motive in first violin, and other instruments. The movement closes with a fugato with a C pedal or organ point.

2. Ravel, *Piano Trio in A Minor*, Third Movement.
3. Dello Joio, *Concerto for Harp and Orchestra*, First Movement.
4. Webern, *Passacaglia for Orchestra Op. 1*.

5. Copland, *Passacaglia.*
6. Piston, *Passacaglia.*
7. Lukas Foss, *Passacaglia.*

A four-measure theme presented in the left hand is followed by 20 repetitions. The theme is in the top voice in Variation 13, and canonic imitation appears in Variations 16, 17, 18.

8. Hindemith, *Symphonie, "Harmonie du Welt."*
9. Reger, *Introduction, Passacaglia and Fugue for Two Pianos.*
10. Riegger, *Symphony No. 3,* Last Movement.
11. Berg, *Wozzeck, Passacaglia* in Act I.

Chaconne

The chaconne, also derived from an old dance, is closely associated with the passacaglia. Both are based on a theme that is constantly repeated. Since the two forms are similar, there has been considerable confusion in labeling and distinguishing them. However, based on the Baroque concept of the passacaglia and chaconne, one basic difference presents itself which helps to clarify the two forms. While the passacaglia is based on a melodic theme that is usually presented alone at the beginning of the composition, the chaconne is based on a harmonic theme. This "theme" is a succession of chords which serve as a harmonic foundation for the music. Thus the texture of the thematic material is the essential difference.

The passacaglia quite naturally parallels the ostinato form, while the chaconne is a type of theme with variations with the various repetitions or variations separated and complete within themselves.

The Bach *Chaconne* from the *Sonata No. 4 for Violin* is an outstanding example of this form. The harmonic theme is:

Bach: *Violin Sonata No. 4, Chaconne*

In order to see how the harmonic theme is varied and modified, the first few measures of each variation are presented here for study.

1. The original bass of the theme is closely followed:

2. A chromatic base line is added:

3. The melody is embellished in a rhythmic pattern:

4. Use of a motive in arpeggio form:

5. Scale-wise movement and skips of chord tones in sixteenth notes:

6. Sequential pattern in sixteenth notes:

7. Sequential pattern with combination of eighth and sixteenth notes:

8. Pattern similar to No. 6 with sixteenth and thirty-second notes:

9. Continuous thirty-second notes in scale-wise movement:

10. Return to sixteenth notes with skips of the diminished seventh chord:

The next four variations return to a more harmonic texture:

15. Scale-wise movement in quicker note values:

The next eight variations are in the parallel key of D major. Notice the uniqueness of each one:

18.

19.

20.

21.

22.

23.

24.

25.

26. Use of arpeggios.

27. Use of scale movement.

28.

29. Similar to the original theme.

A concise example of the chaconne is the William Byrd, *Malt's Come Downe*. A simple harmonic scheme of four measures becomes the foundation and framework for a set of separate variations. The melody, which is organized simply, is primarily scale-wise and is relatively free in each variation with an occasional contour resembling the original melody. The rhythm builds gradually from slower to quicker movement.

Theme

Byrd: *Malt's Come Downe*

Variation I

Variation II—Quarter-note movement in top voice

Variation III—Quarter-note movement in low voice

Variation IV—Quarter-note movement in two voices

Variation V—Eighth notes in top voice

Variation VI—Eighth notes in low voice

Variation VII—Eighth notes in two voices

Variation VIII—A gradual slowing down of motion

ADDITIONAL EXAMPLES OF THE CHACONNE

1. Handel, *Ciacona in D Minor*.

The harmonic theme and the first two measures of each variation will give some insight into various ways of elaborating the harmonic structure:

Theme

Handel: *Ciacona in D Minor*

111

2. Purcell, *Chacony in G Minor for Strings*.
3. Couperin, *Chaconne*.
4. Pachelbel, *Ciaconna*.
5. Brahms, *Symphony No. 4*, Finale.

Theme

Allegro   Brahms: *Symphony No. 4, in E Minor, Finale (Theme)*

The variations are bridged over and are continuous in movement. Listen for the ascending scale-wise melody of the theme as it appears in the upper part and in the bass. Because of the emphasis on the melody in this movement, it is often labeled a passacaglia. However, since the theme is introduced in a harmonic setting, the term chaconne seems more appropriate.

6. Beethoven, *Thirty-Two Variations in C minor.*

An eight-measure harmonic theme is presented at the beginning, followed by 32 variations. A specific rhythmic, harmonic, or melodic pattern is set up and followed consistently throughout each variation. In some of the variations the descending bass line is prominent and serves as a unifying influence. The theme is:

Allegretto (♩ = 100–104)   Beethoven: *Thirty-Two Variations in C Minor*

The Chorale-Prelude

Another type of variation is found in the chorale-prelude. The chorale itself is a German Lutheran hymn introduced by Martin Luther (1483-1546) for congregational singing in church services. The melodies were drawn from secular and sacred sources and were harmonized for mixed voices (soprano, alto, tenor, and bass). The chorale-prelude is a composition for organ, based on a chorale melody and is a variation, or improvisation-like arrangement, of the original melody. It was designed to be performed on the organ before the chorale was sung by the congregation. However, the chorale-preludes have taken their place as solo compositions for organ recital repertoire and as preludes and postludes in the church service. Since the music follows the structure of the chorale melody, the form is free and sectional.

Several general types of chorale-preludes will be discussed and illustrated.

1. A harmonic, or contrapuntal, accompaniment is established and becomes the setting and framework for the chorale melody.

In the Bach chorale-prelude, *Wachet auf ruft uns die Stimme* *(Sleepers Awake, a Voice is Calling),* from the *Cantata No. 147,* a melodic and rhythmic motive is set up for the first 12 measures. The chorale melody is then added to this accompaniment. This elaborate accompaniment alternates alone and in combination with the chorale melody. The first three phrases of the chorale are:

Bach: *Wachet auf ruft uns die Stimme*

Johann Walther, in his chorale-prelude *Wer nur lieben Gott lasst walten* (If Thou but Suffer God to Guide Thee) illustrates another example of this type of chorale-prelude. A two-voiced accompaniment in free canonic imitation serves as the background for the chorale melody. The first two phrases of the chorale melody are:

Walther: *Wer nur lieben Gott lasst walten*

2. A second general type of chorale-prelude is a melodic embellishment of the chorale melody itself. The Bach chorale-prelude, *O Mensch, bewein' dein' Sunde gross* (O Man, Bewail Thy Grievous Fall), is illustrative of this type of variation. The first three phrases of the chorale and chorale-prelude are presented for comparison:

Bach: *O Mensch, bewein' dein Sunde gross*

The notes of the chorale melody are circled:

119

3. A third type of chorale-prelude is the use of some fugal treatment of each phrase of the chorale. In the Bach chorale-prelude, *Wir glauben all' an einen Gott* (We Believe in One God), each phrase appears in fugal imitation.

Chorale: Bach: *Wir glauben all' an einen Gott*

Moderato ma energico (♩ = 60)

An interesting type of chorale-prelude of this general type is the *In Dulci Jubilo* of Bach. Both the chorale melody and the triplet accompaniment pattern appear in canon form:

Bach: *In Dulci Jubilo*

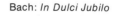

(*4 ft. Reed Stop*)

ADDITIONAL EXAMPLES OF THE CHORALE-PRELUDE

1. Flor Peeters, *Chorale Preludes for Organ Op. 68 and Op. 70.*
2. Johann Walther, *"Wer nur den lieben Gott"*
3. Bach,
   Herzlich thut mich verlangen.
   Schmucke dicke, O Liebe Seele.
4. Brahms, *Chorale Preludes for Organ.*
5. Franck,
   Chorale No. 1 in E major.
   Chorale No. 3 in A minor.
6. Wagner, *Die Meistersinger, Church Scene* in Act I.
7. Healey Willan, *Six Chorale Preludes.*
8. Cowell, *Three Ostinati with Chorales.*

Theme and Variations

Closely related to the chaconne, with its stated theme followed by a series of variations, is the *theme and variation* form. It is the most familiar kind of composition employing the variation principle and is no doubt the easiest form to recognize. Its general plan is a statement of the theme in a simple, direct manner, followed by a number of variations, each variation offering a new and distinctive treatment of the theme, either rhythmically, harmonically, or melodically. The theme is usually a two- or three-part form and the variations range from small and simple changes and modifications to large, extended, and complex ones. Like all forms in music, it has increased in length and intricacy as it has developed.

One of the earliest examples of the variation idea and principle is found in some of the early Masses, in which a plain song melody becomes the basis and principal melodic material for all the movements or sections of the Mass and is altered and varied either rhythmically or melodically in each movement. The *Missa Pange Lingua* of Des Prés is an example.

The French word *double* is an eighteenth-century term for a simple kind of variation. It is usually found in certain movements and dances of the Baroque suite, in which a sarabande or gavotte is repeated in a more elaborate and ornamental version. It consists mainly of embellishments of the original dance movement. The Sarabande from the Bach, *English Suite No. 3 in G minor* illustrates this type of variation. The Sarabande is presented in the Suite, followed by its variation or double. The first eight measures of each are given here for study and comparison:

Bach: *English Suite No. 3 in G Minor, Sarabande*

Les agréments de la même Sarabande

There are two main types of the theme-and-variation form. The first is a small variation form which presents a short theme, often in two parts, which is followed by separate variations based on the theme. It follows the same basic plan as the chaconne with its theme (harmonic) and separate variations. However, the small variation form is usually more concerned with the melody of the theme and with its elaboration and embellishment. A well-known example is the variations of Handel, *Air with Variations* ("The Harmonious Blacksmith"). A simple theme in two parts (AB) is stated, followed by five separate variations. In Variation I the melody is embellished in sixteenth notes which outline the underlying harmony. In Variation II an Alberti bass supplies an accompaniment in the left hand and the melody alternates between the inner voice and the stationary tone B in the right hand. A triplet figure embellishes the melody in Variation III, with broken chords outlining the harmony in the left. In Variation IV the triplets appear in the left hand, but they assume an accompanying role here while the melody appears in somewhat altered form in the right hand. Rapid scale passages in thirty-second notes are used throughout Variation V, except at the cadences. Part A of the theme and its variations are presented here:

Theme

Andante moderato

Handel: *The Harmonious Blacksmith*

Variation I

Variation II

Variation III

second time **pp**

Variation IV

Variation V

Even though this type of variation is characteristic of the classic period, many composers of later periods employed the same basic design and framework. For example, the second movement of Schubert's *String Quartet in D minor* is a theme with variations. The theme is the melody from the Schubert song, *Death and the Maiden*. Five variations follow the statement of the theme. Notice the rhythmic pattern of the theme:

Schubert: *String Quartet In D Minor, Second Movement*

A brief outline of the rhythm for each variation is given below:

Variation I

first violin   obligato

second violin
and
viola

cello   basic rhythm of
the theme

Basic Forms in Music

Variation II

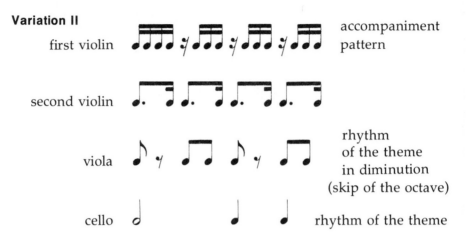

first violin — accompaniment pattern

second violin

viola — rhythm of the theme in diminution (skip of the octave)

cello — rhythm of the theme

Variation III

Harmony is the same as in Variation II, but the rhythm is changed to:

Brief imitation appears between the first violin and cello.

Variation IV—Parallel major key

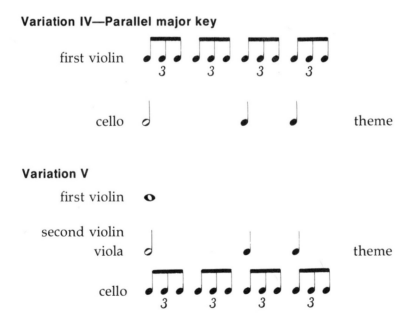

first violin

cello — theme

Variation V

first violin

second violin
viola — theme

cello

In Variation V, after two measures, the rhythm ♫♫ appears in the first violin and is joined later by the second violin and viola. In the coda, this rhythm changes to ♩. ♪ ♪ and gradually "unwinds" to ♪ ♪ and a return to the original rhythm of the theme ♩ ♩ ♩ .

ADDITIONAL EXAMPLES OF THE VARIATION FORM

1. Handel, *Suite in D minor, Aria and Variations.*

This composition illustrates some simple techniques for varying a theme. The theme is presented in a simple harmonic context. The first variation embellishes the melody with sixteenth notes, with some harmonic change and more rhythmic activity in the left hand. In Variation II, a sixteenth-note figure in the left hand embellishes the original bass part. A sixteenth-note pattern appears in the inner voice in Variation III, a triplet figure in the bass in Variation IV, two-voiced counterpoint in Variation V, and a rhythmic pattern ♪ ♫♫ in Variation VI.

2. Mozart, *Piano Sonata in D Major K.284,* Third Movement.

The theme is a three-part form. There are 12 variations, each of which is unique and offers some new treatment of the melody, harmony, or rhythm.

3. Mozart, *Six Variations on the folk song, Ah! Vous dirai-je, Maman.*
   The theme is a three-part form.
4. Mozart, *Sonata for Violin and Piano K.31,* Second Movement.
5. Byrd, *Carman's Whistle.*
6. Rameau, *Gavotte Variée.*
7. Haydn, *String Quartet Op. 76 No. 3,* Second Movement.
8. Bach, *Goldberg Variations.*
9. Mendelssohn, *Variations Serieuses.*

The second type of theme and variation form originated in the nineteenth century. It is a larger and more complex form, quite free in concept and structure, and is more extended and continuous than the former type. Often there are no formal and clear breaks between the variations. There is considerable latitude and freedom in the use of the theme, and the idea of variation is applied in the widest sense. Emphasis is on the structural unity of the composition rather than the variation of the theme itself. Many times, only the large general outline of the theme is retained and the aural recognition of the theme is negligible. Even though both types of the theme and variation form can be found in all periods of music, this latter type is characteristic of the romantic, post-romantic, and contemporary periods.

This large variation form was greatly influenced by Beethoven, whose chief contribution to the form was variety of keys, use of two themes, and a freer, more creative approach to the development of the theme.

The last movement of the Beethoven *Symphony No. 3 in E♭ Major* *("Eroica"),* illustrates this form. The movement opens with 11 measures of introduction. The first theme is initially heard simply and in unison. It is a framework upon which Beethoven developed the movement.

Beethoven: *Symphony No. 3*
in E♭ Major ("Eroica"), Last Movement

Allegro molto

Variations I and II offer a contrapuntal treatment of the theme. The counterpoint creates rhythmic movement by moving from eighth notes to triplets:

Variation I

Variation II

There are no real breaks after these two variations, and the composition becomes a continuous whole.

Variation III

A new (second) theme is introduced in the woodwinds, with the

130

first theme serving as the bass part. (For more clarity in the remaining analysis of this movement, the first theme will be called the bass theme and the second the melodic theme.) The sixteenth-note counterpoint in the strings increases the rhythmic motion from the two previous variations.

Melodic theme

Bass theme

Variation IV

The first four notes of the bass theme are given fugal treatment, with the counterpoint taken from Variation I. The key is the relative minor (C minor):

Variation V

Both themes appear as in Variation III, beginning in B minor and closing in D major.

Variation VI

The first four notes of the bass theme become the background for a new dance-like rhythm (♩ ♫ | ♩ ♫) in G minor.

Variation VII

Both the bass and melodic themes appear together in C major and are repeated in the parallel key, where they are reversed (double counterpoint). The variation ends on a dominant seventh chord on B♭, which prepares and introduces the key of E♭ major for the next variation. This key remains for the rest of the movement.

Variation VIII

The bass theme is given fugal treatment and is inverted. An altered version of the melodic theme appears later on.

Variation IX

A harmonized version of the melodic theme with a change of tempo. Triplets are introduced as an accompaniment pattern later in the variation, anticipating the same rhythm in the next variation.

Variation X

Triplet arpeggios in the strings accompany the melodic theme.

Coda

The coda is in several sections. The last one brings back the melodic theme in a quick tempo.

A unique and complex example of the variation form of the second type is the Franck, *Variations Symphoniques* for piano and orchestra. Three basic themes furnish the material for the variations, which are organized in a continuous and unified whole. The music is improvisational in style and extremely free in design and structure. Any one of the themes may appear alone in the piano or orchestral part, as a fragment or motive, antiphonally, in short "development" sections, and in various keys—all in an original and novel treatment:

Introductory Theme

Franck: *Variations Symphoniques*

Theme I

Theme II

SUMMARY

The variation principle plays an important role in music of all styles and periods. Its presence ranges from a simple or slight alteration of a melody to a large structural change of a theme harmonically, rhythmically, or melodically.

In the Baroque period the bass ostinato or ground bass served as a unifying influence in the music. A short motive was repeated consecutively in the bass, with new material added above.

Even though there is considerable confusion concerning the passacaglia and chaconne, for all practical purposes it can be said that the passacaglia is usually a melodic theme and the chaconne a harmonic theme. Both become the basis for a series of variations.

The theme and variation form appears to fall into two main classifications. The first is the simple type, where a theme is stated, followed by any number of separate and distinct variations. In these variations the melody may be embellished by arpeggios, rapid scale passages, broken chords, trills, and the like. Or there may be certain alterations harmonically, rhythmically, and contrapuntally or some combination of these techniques. The second and larger type of variation is a much freer and more flexible application of the variation principle. Influenced by Beethoven and continued by Brahms, Schumann, and others, it was conceived as a creative rather than an imitative treatment of the theme. The theme frequently serves as the germ of an idea or as a point of departure for an extended composition. Most often the variations are not heard as separate units but merge into a unified and ongoing whole.

ADDITIONAL EXAMPLES OF VARIATIONS
1. Brahms, *Variations on a Theme by Handel.*
2. Brahms, *Variations on a Theme by Haydn.*
3. Schumann, *Etudes Symphoniques.*
4. D'Indy, *Istar Variations Op. 42.*
5. Beethoven, *Symphony No. 5*, Andante.
6. Elgar, *Enigma Variations.*
7. Stravinsky, *Octet for Wind Instruments, Second Movement.*
8. Vaughan Williams, *Fantasia on a Theme by Thomas Tallis.*
9. Copland, *Variations for Piano.*

In a contemporary example of the variation form, Copland places the simplest version of the theme second, causing the "real" statement of the theme to be in the position of the first variation. Apparently he desired a more striking version of the theme in its initial appearance.

10. Strauss, *Don Quixote Op. 35.*
11. Ravel, *Bolero.*
12. Dohnanyi, *Variations on a Nursery Tune Op. 25.*

CHAPTER 6

Forms

in

Polyphonic

Style

Th> here are two general textures in music. One is the vertical, or harmonic, where the musical sounds are organized to produce chords and harmony. This is sometimes referred to as "accompanied melody" and is the use of a melody against a harmonic background. It is the homophonic or chordal style of writing. When music is written as a combination of several simultaneous voices or melodies, it is called polyphonic or contrapuntal and is the horizontal approach to writing. Separate melodic lines combine to create a horizontal sound to the music.

Even though one of these textures may be emphasized and stressed in a composition, it is often difficult to completely separate and differentiate between the two textures. There is usually an underlying harmonic basis to polyphonic writing and there is horizontal movement in a primarily harmonic and chordal composition. It is a matter of emphasis rather than complete separation.

Neither homophonic or polyphonic texture is a form or design in music; rather, it is a process or procedure for presenting musical materials. Both textures have been used separately or in combination throughout all the forms discussed in this book. However, there are certain types of compositions which are written in the polyphonic style and these are highlighted and illustrated in this chapter.

*Canon**

Since the Middle Ages, composers have employed the principle of repetition by some kind of imitation between two or more voices. One particular type is called the canon in which a melody is duplicated at any pitch or time interval. The melody, which begins the canon, is called the leader or dux, and the second voice, which imitates it note for note at a later time interval or at any harmonic interval, is called the follower or comes. The imitation may follow in strict repetition (where all the intervals are of the same quality), or it may be somewhat free. Refer to the early canon, *"Sumer is icumen in"* in Chapter 5.

EXAMPLES OF THE CANON

1. A canon may continue throughout the entire composition. A simple example is the three-voiced canon by Byrd, *Hey Ho.*

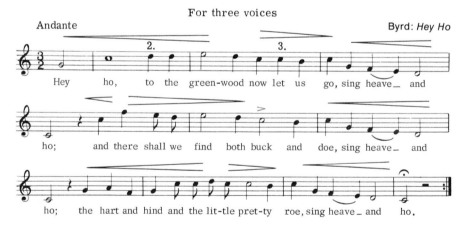

For three voices

Andante — Byrd: *Hey Ho*

Hey ho, to the green-wood now let us go, sing heave and

ho; and there shall we find both buck and doe, sing heave and

ho; the hart and hind and the lit-tle pret-ty roe, sing heave and ho.

* In a round the imitation is limited to the unison or octave while in the canon the imitation may be at any interval.

2. Quite often, folk songs can be used as canons, or rounds. For example, in the following Bohemian folk song, the second voice may begin after the leader has completed the first measure:

3. Bach employs the canon in a consistent and unique way in the *Goldberg Variations*. Every third variation is a canon, each beginning at a different interval progressing from the unison to the ninth. Several of the variations are presented here for illustration:

Variation III—Canon at the unison

Variation VI—Canon at the second

Variation IX—Canon at the third below

Variation XII—Canon at the fourth below. The second voice states the melody in contrary motion (inversion)

4. The chorale-prelude, *In Dulci Jubilo* by Bach (see page 121) is an example of a double canon. The chorale melody is treated as a canon and so is the accompaniment pattern in triplets.

Composers often use the canonic device for short passages or sections in strict or free imitation as a part of a larger composition. It is called canonic imitation.

1. Beethoven writes a three-voiced canon in the trio section of the third movement of his *Sonata for Violin and Piano Op. 96:*

Beethoven:
*Sonata for Violin and Piano,
Op. 96, Third Movement*

2. In the *Farandole* from *L'Arlesienne Suite* by Bizet, the theme appears in canonic imitation after its initial statement:

Bizet: *L'Arlesienne Suite, Farandole*

Tempo di Marcia

3. The first theme of the Franck, *Violin and Piano Sonata* (Last Movement) appears in canonic imitation. The theme, announced at the beginning in the piano, is imitated in the violin part.

Franck: *Violin and Piano Sonata, Last Movement*

When the theme returns, it is heard in the violin and imitated in the piano part.

4. In the Brahms *Piano Sonata in F Minor Op. 5,* the melody in the right hand imitates the left hand part in augmentation (longer note values):

Brahms: *Piano Sonata in F Minor Op. 5*

5. In the Bach *Prelude No. 8 in D♯ Minor* from *The Well Tempered Clavier, Book II,* the top voice is reproduced in the tenor part simultaneously in contrary motion. This is called a "mirror" canon:

Bach: *The Well Tempered Clavier, Book II, Prelude No. 8 in D♯ Minor*

Three other types of canon should be mentioned briefly.

1. *Crab canon*—The original melody is repeated backwards, beginning with the last note and ending with the first. See the retrograde canon in *The Musical Offering* of Bach.

2. *Perpetual canon*—The final cadence is the same as the first measure of the canon, permitting an endless repetition of the music.

3. *Enigma canon*—Only the single melody is written out, and the entrance of the other voice or voices is left to the performer.

141

ADDITIONAL SUGGESTIONS FOR CANON AND CANONIC IMITATION

1. Mozart, *Adagio for Two Horns and Bassoon*, K.410.
2. Brahms, *Canon for Women's Voices*.
3. Hindemith, *Sonata for Two Pianos*, Third Movement.
4. Schoenberg, *Pierrot Lunaire No. 18*.
   A four-part, double canon.
5. Haydn, *String Quartet Op. 76 No. 2*, Third Movement.
6. Bach, *Sonata for Violin and Piano No. 2*, Third Movement.
7. Bartok, *String Quartet No. 4*, First Movement.
8. Schoenberg, *Variations for Orchestra Op. 31*, Variations Nos. 2 and 8.
9. Schumann, *Album for the Young Op. 68, No. 27*.
10. Thomson, *Agnus Dei for Three Voices*.
11. Palestrina, *Missa Brevis, Agnus Dei*.
    A five-voiced motet (sopranos I and II, alto, tenor, and bass).
    Soprano II follows soprano I after two measures in a canon; the other voices move in free imitation.

The Motet and Madrigal

The polyphonic style flourished in the fifteenth, sixteenth, and seventeenth centuries and reached its climax in the works of Palestrina, Victoria, and Lassus in the Renaissance. An outgrowth of this type of writing was the *motet*, which is an a cappella choral composition based on a religious text. Its structure is dependent on the words and is free in design. Even though imitative treatment is identified with the motet, a mixture of homophonic and polyphonic textures is frequently found.

The Lassus *Benedictus* is a two-voiced motet in the mixolydian mode (GABCDEFG). The first motive is imitated at the fourth, a motive in the tenor (measure 7) is imitated at the fifth, and the motive in the cantus (measure 12) is imitated at the octave and returns to imitation at the fifth (measure 16).

Lassus: *Benedictus*

Two motives appear in this motet from the *Missa Brevis* of Palestrina. The first is in the soprano voice at the beginning and the second one is in the tenor in measure 17. Notice the imitation throughout.

Palestrina: *Missa Brevis, Benedictus*

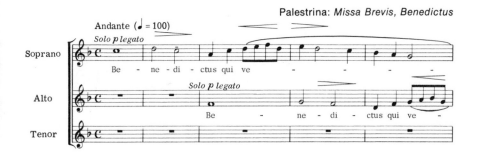

143

In the Baroque period, solo voices and instrumental accompaniments were often added to the choral parts in the motets, which became closely identified with the cantata and other types of church music. Bach wrote six motets, four of them for eight voices. The best known perhaps is *Sing Ye to the Lord* (Singet dem Herrn).

An example of the motet in the classical period is the familiar Mozart, *Ave Verum Corpus*. It combines both the homophonic and polyphonic textures and divides naturally into three parts. The third part begins with imitation between the upper and lower voices.

145

A contemporary example of the motet can be found in the *Missa Brevis* of Kodaly. In the beginning of the Sanctus, a motive is presented in the second alto, followed by its imitation in the other voices:

Kodaly: *Missa Brevis, Sanctus*

The madrigal is also a polyphonic part song. It developed after the motet in the works of Gesualdo, Monteverdi, and Morley. Its chief distinction is that the words for the motet are religious, while those for the madrigal are secular. Both are a *style* of writing rather than a *form*.

146

A madrigal that combines the homophonic and polyphonic textures is *Such as in Love,* by Whythorne, for three voices:

Whythorne: *Such as in Love*

The Invention

Bach gave the name *invention** to 15 short pieces in two voices and 15 in three voices. The term was first used by Bonporti some years earlier as a name for some partitas for violin and figured bass. The Bach *Inventions,* which are "studies in double or triple counterpoint," treat a fairly simple melodic motive in various kinds of imitation. They serve as excellent preliminary exercises in preparation for the study of the fugue. Each uses the music materials uniquely. The *Invention No. 1,* in two voices, illustrates this contrapuntal process. The entire *Invention* is based on the beginning motive in the right hand:

Section I—measures 1-7

The basic motive is imitated at the octave in the first measure and repeats at the fifth in measure 2.

The first four notes of the motive appear in augmentation (double note values) in the left hand (measure 3), and the motive is inverted (contrary motion) in the right, followed by repetition in sequence (duplication of motive on different pitches). This section ends with a complete cadence in the dominant key.

Section II—measures 7-15

The first two measures of Section I are repeated in G major, with the voices reversed in double counterpoint. In measures 9-10 the motive is heard in contrary motion and in sequence. Each time, it is imitated a fifth above. Measures 11-12 are a repetition of measures 3-4 on different pitches and in double counterpoint, with the voices reversed. The section ends with a cadence in the relative minor key of A.

Section III—measures 15 to the end

In measures 15-18 the motive is imitated in the second voice and alternates between its original form and contrary motion. Measures 19-20 are quite similar to measures 3-4, except for the contrary motion. The invention ends with a strong cadence in the tonic key.

---

* The style of the invention somewhat resembles the style of the preludes from *The Well-Tempered Clavier*.

Forms in Polyphonic Style

Bach: *Two-Part Invention No. 1*

The Bach *Two-part Inventions* are an excellent illustration of the use of imitation and other contrapuntal devices. See Numbers 2 and 8 for canonic imitation and Number 6 for double counterpoint (measures 1-4 and 5-8).

The Fugue

Imitative counterpoint was a basic characteristic of the sixteenth-century motet and continued its development with the instrumental fantasia of the early seventeenth century (Byrd and Gibbons), the ricerar (imitative treatment of several rather slow themes in succession), and the canzona, which used a variety of textures but stressed polyphonic treatment of themes and motives. The canzona paved the way for the fully developed fugue of Bach.

The fugue (from the word *fuga,* meaning flight) is a contrapuntal composition consisting of a melody, called a subject, which appears alone and is then imitated by all the parts or voices in close succession, with each voice continuing with a counter-subject or "counter-melodies." The first imitation is called the answer, or response, and consists of the subject transposed a fourth or a fifth higher (it is always determined from above even though the answer may actually sound below the subject). The exposition of the fugue consists of the presentation of the subject or answer in all the voices and usually ends with some kind of cadence. A development section follows in which new material may be added, and the subject is "developed" by various contrapuntal devices and modulations. There is a return to the original tonic key and usually a statement of the subject. A coda is sometimes added as an extended cadence. Fugues usually divide quite naturally into sections that are defined by cadences, new material, and changes in style. Any section or connecting passage that does not contain a complete statement of the subject is called an episode. Unity is achieved in the fugue by the continuous use of the same material (subject), and variety is gained by diversity of treatment and material.

EXAMPLES OF THE FUGUE

1. Bach, *The Well-Tempered Clavier, Book II, Fugue No. 5 in D Major.*

The exposition of this fugue consists of the first 10 measures. The subject appears in measure 1 and is answered (imitated) in measure 2 a fifth above the subject. This consistent use of the fifth in the answer forms a "real" answer, or response. The subject is presented again in measure 5, followed by the answer in measure 6. It is a four-voiced fugue and may be compared to the four vocal voices (soprano, alto, tenor, and bass). The outline for the exposition is as follows:

Subject (tenor) measures 1-2

Answer (alto) measures 2-3

The first voice (tenor) continues its melodic line (counterpoint) with a motive taken from the end of the subject:

Episode (measure 4):

The above motive appears in imitation

Subject (soprano) measure 5

Answer (bass) measure 6

The answer is introduced before the completion of the subject. This overlapping is called stretto.

Basic Forms in Music

An episode brings the exposition to a close (measure 7-10).

The rest of the fugue is divided into a number of sections (marked in the musical score), each ending on a cadence. The chief contrapuntal device used throughout is stretto, in which the subject is imitated in close succession. It appears in two voices in measure 14, in three voices in measures 21 and 28 and 33, and finally in all four voices in measure 44. The four-note basic motive derived from the subject becomes an integral part of the fugue's development and serves as a unifying influence for the entire fugue as an accompaniment and as stretto in episodes (measures 16-20 and 35-39).

Bach: *The Well Tempered Clavier, Book II, Fugue No. 5 in D Major*

Section IV

Stretto

Section V

Stretto

Section VI

Stretto

Section VII

Section VIII

Stretto

2. Bach, *Well Tempered Clavier, Book II, Fugue No. 6 in D Minor.*

This is a three-voiced fugue with the subject presented alone in the first two measures. The answer (real) imitates the subject at the fifth in measure 3. After one measure of episode (measure 5), the subject returns, followed by an episode to the cadence ending the exposition in measure 10.

Bach: *The Well Tempered Clavier,*
Book II, Fugue No. 6 in D Minor

The development section (measure 10) opens with a motive (triplets) from the subject in contrary motion (inversion) in the top voice, followed by a complete announcement of the subject in D minor. Fragments of the subject appear in the other voices:

In measure 17 the subject is heard in contrary motion (inversion) and in stretto. Subject begins in the middle voice on the dominant tone (A) and on the tonic tone (D) in the low voice a beat later (circled notes).

After an episode based on the triplet figure of the subject, a complete announcement of the subject serves as a codetta, ending the fugue.

3. Bach, *The Well-Tempered Clavier, Book II, Fugue No. 3 in C Minor.*

This is a three-voiced fugue with a fourth voice added for reinforcement in the last section (measure 19). A one-measure subject appears alone at the beginning, followed by its answer in measure 2. The first note of the subject "answers" at the fourth (G to C) in order to maintain the C minor tonality. The rest of the answer is a fifth above the subject. The answer is tonal when any note of the subject is imitated at the fourth:

Bach: *The Well Tempered Clavier, Book II, Fugue No. 3 in C Minor*

An interesting and unusual passage appears in measures 14-15, where the subject is heard an octave above its initial statement in the top voice, accompanied by the subject underneath in stretto and augmentation (quarter notes instead of eighths). In measure 15 the low voice introduces the subject in free inversion (contrary motion). Thus, in two measures three contrapuntal devices are heard: stretto, augmentation, and contrary motion:

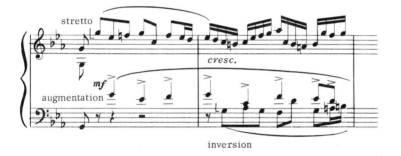

Later on, the subject appears in augmentation in the low voice:

In the last section, the codetta, stretto is used again:

4. Hindemith, *Fugue in F* from *Ludus Tonalis*.

This contemporary fugue follows the general plan of the traditional fugue quite closely, but is freer in organization. For example, while the answer in a traditional fugue is an imitation of the subject at the fourth or fifth, in a contemporary fugue it may begin on any tone.

EXPOSITION

In this three-voiced fugue, the subject is stated in the first six measures alone, followed by an answer at the sixth (third below). The accompanying voice uses several short motives in sequence. The subject is heard in the inner voice in measure 13 and the exposition ends in measure 19.

The rest of the fugue is sectional in structure and employs several contrapuntal devices. Following a short episode (measures 19-22), the subject appears in contrary motion (inversion) in the top voice and a measure later in the low voice in stretto. After an announcement of the subject in retrograde in the middle voice (measure 42), and a chromatic and sequential episode, the subject returns in retrograde again (measure 54) to close the fugue.

The Double Fugue

The Kyrie Eleison from the *Requiem Mass in D Minor* by Mozart is a double fugue which has two subjects instead of one. Subject A is stated in the bass at the beginning of the fugue and Subject B follows in the alto in measure 2. This illustrates the type of double fugue in which the two subjects appear together at the beginning in different voices. Answer A (tonal) is heard in the soprano in measure 4, followed by Answer B (real) in the tenor in measure 5. Subject A is announced again in the alto in measure 8 with Subject B in the bass in the following measure. The exposition is completed with Answer A in the tenor (measure 11) and Answer B in the soprano (measure 12). Each voice has stated the subject or answer A and the subject or answer B. The score for the exposition of the fugue is given for study and analysis:

Mozart: *Requiem Mass in D Minor, Kyrie Eleison*

During the rest of the fugue the two subjects usually appear together in various voices and keys. Stretto is found in soprano and bass voices with subject A (measures 27-32), and in all four voices with Subject B (measures 33-37 and 44-48).

When a passage in a composition employs fugal procedures and is written in a fugal style, it is called a *fugato*. This type of writing often appears in development sections of symphonies, sonatas, etc. A short fugue, which contains an exposition and an additional section, is called a *fughetta*.

SUMMARY

Polyphonic texture in music implies the use of two or more simultaneous melodies (horizontal movement) in contrast to homophonic and chordal texture (vertical). These two textures may be separate and distinct or they may be combined in a composition. They do not constitute a form, but are a process or procedure.

The basic element in all polyphonic writing is imitation. Occasionally the melodies are independent and unrelated in structure, but more often they are organized and arranged with some type of imitation. Various uses of imitation are found in the canon, motet and madrigal, invention, fugue, and double fugue. Unity is achieved by the repetition of the same material—a theme, motive, or subject. Variety is met by various kinds of treatment of the theme and new material. The most frequently used contrapuntal devices are stretto, augmentation, contrary motion (inversion), and double counterpoint.

ADDITIONAL EXAMPLES OF POLYPHONY

1. Bach, *Two- and Three-part Inventions.*

Each is unique in its treatment of motive and in the use of contrapuntal devices.

2. Bach, *Fugues* from *The Well Tempered Clavier, Books I* and *II.*

3. Bach, *G Minor ("Little") Fugue for Organ.*

4. Bach, *The Art of the Fugue.*

5. Bach, *Toccatas and Fugues.*

6. Mozart, *Adagio and Fugue in C Minor, K.546.*

7. Handel, *And with His Stripes,* from the *Messiah* (fugue).

8. Haydn, *Awake the Harp,* from *The Creation* (fugue).

9. Haydn, *Achieved Is the Glorious Work,* from *The Creation* (double fugue).

10. Brahms, *But the Righteous Souls Are in the Hands of God,* from *German Requiem,* Part I (fugue).

A pedal point on D (tonic) appears throughout the entire fugue.

11. Mendelssohn, *Overture* to *Elijah* (fugue).

12. Franck, *Prelude, Chorale, and Fugue.*

13. Bloch, *Concerto Grosso,* finale (fugue).

14. Hindemith, *Sonata for Two Pianos,* Fifth Movement (fugue).

15. Vaughan Williams, *Symphony in F Minor,* Finale (fugue).

16. Bartok, *Music for Strings, Percussion and Celeste,* First Movement.

17. Stravinsky, *Symphony of Psalms,* Second Movement (fugue).

18. Hindemith, *String Quartet No. 4,* First Movement.

This illustrates a type of double fugue in which each of the two subjects has its own exposition followed by a development section, where they are combined in various arrangements.

Section I—Exposition I
Subject I
All four instruments state the first four notes, and the viola continues.
Answer I
first violins
Subject I
second violin
Answer I
cello after two "false entries"

A statement of the subject (on F♯) in second violin, viola, and cello and an episode and a stretto treatment combining all instruments, bring this section to a close.

Section II—Exposition II

Subject II—first violin with contrapuntal accompaniment in viola

Answer II—second violin with counterpoint in first violin

Subject II—cello with counterpoint in first violin

Answer II—

After the subject appears several times in stretto, this section ends with a cadenza based on the triplet figure of the subject.

Section III—Development

After the cadenza, Subject I is heard again, followed by the combination of the two subjects with the original counterpoint.

The exposition of Subject I (first exposition) is repeated and a final statement of Subject I ends the movement.

CHAPTER 7

The Sonata and Sonata-Allegro Form

T he term *sonata* (from the word *sonare*, meaning "to sound") has two different meanings. The first meaning generally refers to a composition of three or four movements for solo instruments in contrasting style, key, and tempo. The second refers to the form of one of the movements (usually the first) of the sonata and is called the *sonata-allegro form*. The development of the sonata is an interesting and influential one in the history of music, but it is not within the scope of this book. A brief look into the development of the sonata, however, will give some background and insight into the sonata-allegro form, which is our main concern in this chapter. Just as the sonata form became freer and more complex in its design and organization through the years, so the sonata-allegro form was altered and transformed in concept and structure.

The term *sonata* in the Renaissance period indicated any composition written for instruments, in contrast to the vocal form called the cantata.

The sonata in the Baroque period was a composition usually in four movements consisting of a slow introduction, a fugal allegro movement, a lyric slow movement, and a quick dance-like finale. The interest and development of the sonata in this period was due to the popularity and prominence given to the strings in the seventeenth century. J. S. Bach wrote a number of these sonatas for violin, cello, viol da gamba, and flute, separately or in combination and with or without harpsichord accompaniment. The Bach *Sonata for Violin and Clavier, No. 3 in E Major,* is an example of this type of sonata. It has four movements and follows the general plan of the Baroque sonata, as was stated above. The term sonata was also used in this period by Scarlatti in his short one-movement sonatas for harpsichord written in binary form. Carl Philip Emanuel Bach experimented with the sonata form and emphasized the homophonic style instead of the earlier polyphonic texture. His sonatas were innovative, with special attention given to the development of material, to changes in tempo and keys, a general extension of the form into sections, and an emphasis on tonic and dominant relationships. These characteristics were all elements that were to be refined and extended as components of the sonata-allegro form.

The sonata form was perfected in the Classical period with Haydn, Mozart, and Beethoven. It consisted mainly of four movements, the first usually in sonata-allegro form (which will be discussed and illustrated later in this chapter), a slow movement often ternary in design, the Song Form and Trio (minuetto or scherzo and trio) and a fast movement in rondo or sonata-allegro form. These forms of the movements are only general ones, as there are many exceptions and differences in structure and design. Except for the sonata-allegro form, the others have all been explained and illustrated in previous chapters. The terms sonata, symphony, concerto, quartet, etc., all refer to this same grouping of movements. For example, a symphony is a sonata for symphony orchestra, a string quartet is a sonata for four string instruments, and a concerto is a sonata for solo instrument and orchestra. In the Romantic period the sonata extended the fundamental idea of the classic form into freer use of tonality, occasionally a pictorial or programmatic basis, changes in order of movements, the use of cyclic technique and a tendency toward the use of motives and small fragments instead of a theme.

The second use of the term sonata is that of the form of one of the movements of the sonata, symphony, string quartet, concerto, etc. This is the sonata-allegro form and is found most often as the first movement of the sonata, but it may be the design of other movements or of any type of composition as well. As was suggested earlier in a consideration of the sonata form, C.P.E. Bach was most influential in the development of this form. One discovers certain innovations and trends in the use of music materials in the first movements of his sonatas, which came to full maturity with Haydn, Mozart, and Beethoven. The use of two contrasting themes in related keys, transitional passages, development and expansion of themes, and a return to the original theme are some of these innovations and characteristics.

The basic design of the sonata-allegro form in the Classic period is an expansion and extension of the ternary form. Its form consists of three large sections: exposition, development, and recapitulation, which represents statement, departure, and restatement of material. Its plan is as follows:

Exposition:
    principal theme (tonic key)
    transition
    subordinate theme (dominant)*
    closing theme or section (dominant)

Development:
    The principal or subordinate theme or new material is presented with various contrasts in keys, texture, and treatment.

Recapitulation (this section may be an exact repetition of the exposition or it may be altered and expanded)
    principal theme (tonic)
    transition
    subordinate theme (tonic)
    closing theme or section (tonic)
    coda

The composer sees in the basic structure of the sonata-allegro form a natural and consistent sequence of presenting musical ideas. He presents the thematic material in the exposition, these ideas are developed creatively in the development section, and the themes return in either exact or modified repetition in the recapitulation.

The form has been used as a basic skeleton and outline by composers of the Classic period up to the present and has been altered and adapted to meet their own individual musical needs and style. Thus it is uniform only in its broadest outlines. Each composer treats it in a unique and stylistically appropriate way.

---

* When a composition is in the minor key, the subordinate and closing themes of the exposition are usually in the relative major key.

The first movement of the Beethoven, *Sonata for Piano Op. 49 No. 2* is a clear and concise example of the sonata-allegro form. Its outline is:

Exposition:

  Principal theme in G major (measures 1-12)

  Transition modulating to the dominant key (D) (measures 12-20)

  Subordinate theme in D major (measures 21-36)

  Closing section in D (measures 36-52)

Development:

  A short section stating the principal theme (measures 53-59)

  Transition returning to G major (measures 59-66)

Recapitulation:

  Principal theme in G major (measures 67-75)

  Transition (measures 75-87)

  Subordinate theme in G major (measures 88-103)

  Closing section in G major (measures 103 on)

Beethoven, *Sonata for Piano,*
Op. 49, No. 2, First Movement

Subordinate Theme

Closing Section

Development

Transition

cresc. - - - - - - -

Recapitulation

f

p

Principal Theme

cresc.

Transition

f

Closing Section

EXAMPLES OF THE SONATA-ALLEGRO FORM

1. Mozart, *Sonata for Piano, K.284,* First Movement.
Exposition:
    Principal theme in C major:

Transition modulating to G Major:

Subordinate theme in G Major:

Brief closing section in G Major:

Development:

The principal theme is "developed" in G minor, D minor, and A minor. The second measure of the theme appears as a separate motive sequentially. The closing section material also appears in this section.

Recapitulation:

Principal theme in C major
Transition
Subordinate theme in C major
Closing section

2. Clementi, *Sonatina for Piano Op. 36 No. 5*, First Movement.

The term *sonatina* usually means a shorter and somewhat easier sonata. In this Clementi Sonatina the first movement is in sonata-allegro form. It is a miniature design and is clear and regular.

Exposition:
 Principal Theme in G Major:

 Transition modulating to D Major.
 Subordinate theme in D Major:

The closing section is only an extended cadence of two measures.

Development:

Both themes appear in this section. The subordinate theme is modified.

Recapitulation:

This is an exact repetition of the exposition, except that the section remains in the tonic key throughout.

3. Schubert, *Symphony in B♭ Major No. 5*, First Movement.

Exposition:

Introduction of four measures.

Principal theme in B♭ Major (measures 5-41):

Transition (measures 41-64).

This transition modulates to the dominant key of F major. The motive is based on the principal theme and appears in imitation:

Subordinate theme in F Major (measures 65-80):

Closing section begins in measure 92 after an extended cadence.

Development:
   The first five notes of the principal theme are highlighted, with a slight change in rhythm:

   The section is extended by the use of another motive:

Recapitulation:
   Principal theme in E♭ major. (The subdominant key is used instead of the tonic key.)
   Transition modulating to B♭ major
   Subordinate theme in B♭ major
   Closing section
   Coda
For the most part, the three illustrations of the sonata-allegro form have been clear and distinct and have followed the basic design consistently. However, composers often modify the content with a unique treatment of the music materials. Several of these will be illustrated to show some of the possibilities.

   1. Brahms, *Symphony No. 2*, Op. 73, First Movement.
   In the first movements of his first three symphonies, Brahms employs a motive which appears with the principal theme and becomes an important and significant part of the total structure of the movement. This is called a *basic motive* and appears both alone and in conjunction with the theme.

   Exposition:
   Principal theme in D major
       The principal theme is in two parts. The four-note pattern in the bass at the beginning of the movement (marked by brackets in the musical excerpt) serves as the basic motive for the movement. The two parts of the theme are separated by a short interlude:

Part I

Interlude

Part II

Transition

The basic motive appears in two rhythms:

Subordinate theme begins in F♯ Minor:

Closing section:
This section is extended and enlarged into three main parts. The first uses the basic motive in another rhythm (♪♫), the second features a ground bass, and the third repeats the subordinate theme.

Development:
Both parts of the principal theme appear here along with material derived from the basic motive.

Recapitulation:
Principal theme. (The two parts of the principal theme are heard together in the tonic key.)
Brief transition
Subordinate theme in B minor
Closing section
The three parts are heard again.
Coda
The first part of the principal theme and the basic motive are featured.

2. Mozart, *String Quartet K387*, Last Movement.
In a unique manner, Mozart combines the sonata-allegro and fugue forms in this movement. The two themes are contrapuntal in texture and each becomes a subject for a fugal exposition.

Exposition:
Principal theme in G major
A fugue subject of five notes appears in the second violin, is answered (imitated) in the first violin, is repeated in the cello, and is answered again in the viola.
The subject and answer are:

Transition modulating to D major
Subordinate theme

Another fugue subject is presented in the cello, is answered in the viola, repeated in the second violin, and is answered again in the first violin:

The two subjects then appear together in various voices in double counterpoint. For example:

Closing Theme:

Development
This section opens with a chromatic motive, which is imitated by the various instruments:

The principal theme also appears in imitation.
Recapitulation:
This section begins with the transition from the exposition. The

principal and subordinate themes do not appear separately as originally stated, but are heard together in double counterpoint.

Closing theme in G major

Coda: the chromatic motive of the development section and the principal theme return for the close.

3. Sibelius, *Symphony No. 2 in D Major,* First Movement.

Instead of the usual principal and subordinate themes in the sonata-allegro form, Sibelius substitutes a series of short motives and develops them into a unified whole. The treatment of the thematic material is therefore radically changed from the earlier and more traditional form.

Exposition:

A harmonic motive opens the movement and serves as an introduction:

A series of short motives follows and presents the thematic material of the movement:

(a)

The introduction motive accompanies this motive:

(b)

(c)

These motives are heard in this order in the exposition. The principal climax is the presentation of motive "e" in the woodwinds and brasses, with the introduction motive in the strings as the accompaniment. The exposition ends with the introduction motive alone.

Development:
The section begins with motives "e," "f," and "g," with a scale-wise ostinato figure in the strings; the repetition of "snatches" of these motives constitute the rest of the section.

Recapitulation:
This section parallels somewhat the exposition. Motives "a," "g," and "d" appear in order, moving to a climax with motive "e."
The coda returns to the introduction motive and motive "g."

Examples from Mozart, Brahms, and Sibelius have illustrated certain unique features and variants of the sonata-allegro form. A brief outline of several other possibilities with suggested musical illustrations is given below for study and analysis.

1. Alteration of key scheme.
    (a) Beethoven, *Sonata for Piano (Waldstein)*, First Movement. The subordinate theme is in the mediant key.

(b) Mozart, *Sonata in C Major, K.545*, First Movement.

The principal theme in the recapitulation is in the subdominant key.*

(c) Prokofiev, *Classical Symphony*, First Movement.

The principal theme is in D major in the exposition and appears in C major in the recapitulation.

2. Polyphonic texture.

A fughetta or some fugal treatment is incorporated into the form.

(a) Mozart, Overture to *The Magic Flute*.

(b) Smetana, Overture to *The Bartered Bride*.

(c) Beethoven, *String Quartet Op. 59 No. 3*, Finale.

A fugue in sonata-allegro form.

3. New theme in development section.

(a) Schubert, *Symphony in C Major*, First Movement.

(b) Schumann, *Symphony No. 2 Op. 61*, Second Movement.

New theme substitutes for the development section.

4. Recapitulation without principal theme.

(a) Smetana, Overture to *The Bartered Bride*.

Fugal principal theme is omitted in the recapitulation.

(b) Smetana, *String Quartet ("From My Life")*, First Movement.

5. Recapitualtion without subordinate theme.

(a) Franck *Symphony in D Minor*, Finale.

6. Concerto Allegro.

The first movement often has two expositions, one for the orchestra and one for the solo instrument, with or without accompaniment.

(a) Mendelssohn, *Violin Concerto in E Minor*, First Movement.

(b) Beethoven, *Concertos for Piano and Orchestra Nos. 1, 2, and 3*, First Movements.

7. Double subordinate theme.

(a) Mozart, *Sonata for Piano, K.533*, First Movement.

(b) Beethoven, *Sonatas for Piano, Op. 2 No. 3 and Op. 7*, First Movements.

---

* The same key relationship is found in the Schubert *Symphony No. 5*, First Movement.

ADDITIONAL EXAMPLES OF THE SONATA-ALLEGRO FORM

1. Haydn, *Symphony No. 100 in G Major,* First Movement.
2. Shostakovich, *Symphony No. 9,* First Movement.
3. Barber, Overture to *The School for Scandal.*
4. Franck, *Symphony in D Minor,* First Movement.
5. Alban Berg, *Sonata für Clavier, Op. 1.*
   The basic sonata allegro form is followed quite closely here. Both themes appear in the development section.
6. Copland, *Piano Sonata,* First Movement.

This is a contemporary example of the sonata-allegro form. The basic outline or structure of the form is maintained, but the treatment and organization of themes are considerably expanded and varied. Even though there is a well-defined development section, themes and motives from the themes are developed, extended, and varied freely throughout the movement, offering an inner logic and variety all its own.

Another variant of the sonata-allegro form is the sonatine form. It is a sonata-allegro without the development section. This is not the same as the sonatina, which implies the complete idea of the sonata-allegro but in a miniature and shortened form. The Overture to Mozart's *The Barber of Seville* is an example of the sonatine.

An extended introduction opens the composition.

Exposition:

principal theme in E minor:

Transition
Subordinate theme in G major:

Closing section

Two themes appear in this section; the second is used in the famous crescendo:

185

pp

A very brief interlude leads into the recapitulation, which presents the themes in E minor and E major, respectively. A lively coda ends the overture.

ADDITIONAL EXAMPLES OF THE SONATINE FORM

1. Tschaikowsky, Overture to *The Nutcracker Suite.*
2. Shostakovich, *Symphony Op. 10 No. 1,* Finale.
3. Rossini, Overture to *The Barber of Seville.*
4. Tschaikowsky, *Symphony No. 6 Op. 74,* Finale.
5. Sibelius, *Symphony No. 2 in D Major,* Second Movement.
6. Mozart, Overture to *The Marriage of Figaro.*

The term *enlarged sonatine form* is given to a movement or composition when a development section follows the principal theme in the recapitulation. Brahms used this device in the finales of his *Third* and *Fourth Symphonies.* The second movement of the Beethoven *String Quartet Op. 18 No. 3* is another example.

The rondo sonata form is a hybrid form combining the third rondo and the sonata-allegro forms. A development section is substituted for the C section of the third rondo. An example of this form is the last movement of the *Sonata for Piano,* Op. 27, No. 1 by Beethoven.

SUMMARY

The sonata-allegro form consists of a large ternary design, which divides into three sections: exposition, development, and recapitulation. Its basic structure is the presentation of two themes contrasting in key, character, and style; a development of this material, and a repetition of the themes, either exact or modified, in the same key (tonic). Composers may follow a clear and precise structure and design (classic) or they may vary the content, organization, and treatment of the material in a personal, unique manner. At times, the key scheme may be altered, the recapitulation modified, a new theme may appear in the development section, a theme may be omitted or reduced, or there may be a double principal or subordinate theme. These are only a few of the possible variants of the basic structure.

CHAPTER 8

Other

Forms

n discussing and illustrating the compositions in the previous chapters, we have dealt with specific forms and designs which follow a more or less prescribed presentation of musical materials. Even though each composition has unique and original characteristics, each conforms in general to some basic or preexisting design. There are, however, many compositions that are free in structure and that differ in varying degrees from any formal classification. These are not "free" in the sense of being formless or in lacking organization or structure. They are organized differently. Each composition in this category has its own distinctive procedure for acquiring unity and variety and for maintaining order, balance, and coherence in the music; it does not necessarily follow or adapt to one of the basic molds or patterns. A number of titles are given to these compositions—overture, fantasia, rhapsody, scherzo, caprice, ballade, suite, toccata, and arabesque. Several will be discussed and analyzed in this chapter.

The Overture

The overture (from *ouvrir,* to open), originated in the short instrumental introductions of the early Italian operas. Initially an opera or oratorio would begin without any introduction or with a short flourish of trumpets or some other attention-getter. Soon, however, because of the need for audience preparation for the musical work, introductions acquired greater length and more definite form, culminating in the French overture of Lully and the Italian overture of A. Scarlatti in the seventeenth century. In the Classical period the overture became more or less a fixed form (the sonata-allegro, etc.), but gained greater freedom in structure and design in later periods. Overtures fall into three general categories: the Italian and French models, the Classic or Dramatic, and the Potpourri.

THE ITALIAN AND FRENCH OVERTURES

The Italian overture consists of three sections—fast, slow, fast —and was developed in the Neapolitan school in Italy. Mozart's Overture to the *Abduction from the Seraglio* is organized in this manner. The French overture also consists of three movements, but it is slow, fast, slow. The Overture to Handel's *Messiah* is an example of this type of overture.

A slow harmonic theme with a characteristic dotted rhythm opens the overture:

In the second section a subject is presented alone and then treated fugally:

The slow tempo returns in the last few measures and serves more as a coda to the allegro section than as a separate movement. However, some examples do have extended third sections.

THE CLASSIC OR DRAMATIC OVERTURE

The classic overture was influenced by the development of the symphony and the sonata, and its organization was based on a prevailing design, most often the sonata-allegro (first movement) form. It became more of an integral part of the drama of the main work and "prepared the audience for the plot" in mood and spirit. The Overture to Mozart's *The Marriage of Figaro* illustrates this type of overture and is in sonatine form. The trombones imitate the three knocks on the door of the "Temple of Wisdom" which appears in the opera. Even though this overture type is not in the "free form" category, it is outlined briefly here as a representative example of the overture.

Principal theme

Transition to the dominant key:

Subordinate theme:

Closing theme:

The recapitulation consists of the repetition of the exposition with a coda. The subordinate theme is in the tonic key in this section.

The concert overture appeared in the nineteenth century as an independent composition written in a style similar to the operatic overture, either following a prescribed basic form or in a free design.

THE POTPOURRI OVERTURE

The potpourri overture is general in scope and includes all types of operatic overtures, preludes, and introductions written in free form, which employ themes that are a part of the major work or that are related in some way. The simplest kind is where a series of themes from an opera, operetta, or musical show are presented, such as in the Gilbert and Sullivan operettas and Broadway musicals. Unity is often achieved by the repetition of the first theme, but there is no overall design. A similar but more advanced type of potpourri overture occurs when several themes or motives from the major work are developed in symphonic style. The form is usually sectional, with considerable development of the thematic material.

The Prelude to Wagner's *Tristan and Isolde* is a representative example of this latter type. Four motives from the opera are developed into a unified composition. The motives are:

Isolde motive:

The Glance motive:

Love potion:

Longing for death:

The return of the first motive at the close gives unity and balance to the music.

ADDITIONAL EXAMPLES OF THE OVERTURE

1. Handel, *Rinaldo.*
2. Gluck, *Iphigenia in Tauris.*
   Creates mood of storm for the opera.
3. Haydn, *The Creation.*
   Sets the mood and background for the oratorio.
4. Mozart, *Don Giovanni.*
   Brief reference to the statue music of the last scene.
5. Beethoven, *Leonore Overtures.*
   Incorporate themes from the opera.
6. Rossini, *The Barber of Seville.*
   Sonatine form.
7. Rossini, *William Tell* ("Dawn," "The Storm," "Thanksgiving," and "Call to Arms").
   Four sections depict the life of the Swiss people. The themes are not taken from the opera.
8. Weber, *Der Freischütz.*
9. Weber, *Euryanthe.*
10. Weber, *Oberon.*
11. Wagner, *Die Meistersinger.*
    The three motives of the prelude are combined in a recapitulation section.
12. Berlioz, *Le Carnaval Romain.*

13. Dvorak, *Carnival Overture*.
14. Mendelssohn, Overture to *A Midsummer Night's Dream*.
15. Mendelssohn, *Hebrides Overture*.
16. Brahms, *Academic Festival Overture*.
    A concert overture called "a jolly potpourri of students' songs à la Suppe."
17. Tschaikowsky, *1812 Overture*.

The Symphonic Poem

A new form took shape in the Romantic period with the strong interest in program music and the attempt to portray personal and emotional feelings. This is the symphonic poem, which is an orchestral composition based on an extramusical idea, either pictorial or literary. It is usually a one-movement structure, in contrast to the popular three-or four-movement work and a free form governed by the poetic or narrative idea, rather than a set basic form. Each symphonic poem is individual, free, and unique in organization. Some resemble a single movement of a symphony; others suggest a series of movements within a large one-movement structure.

Liszt, *Les Preludes*.

Liszt first used the term *symphonic poem* in 1848 and with him the new form took shape. He also developed the idea of "transformation of themes" in which a theme was presented in various guises to portray changes in poetic thought. This symphonic poem was inspired by Lamartine's "Meditations Poetiques," which depicts life as a series of preludes ending in death. It is written in one movement but falls quite naturally into four main sections. A brief outline of the themes and sections is given below. However, a detailed analysis of the work is encouraged, as it is most inventive in the presentation and development of themes and in its unity of structure.

Section I—Spring and Love
Theme A:
The three-note pattern, with its characteristic skip of the fourth in measure 3, becomes the basic or germinal motive for the entire composition. The phrase is repeated several times with minor changes:

Andante

Theme B:

Played by trombones, cellos, and basses, with an arpeggiated accompaniment in the strings:

Andante maestoso

Theme C:

This theme is played by the second violins, violas, and cellos and is developed and extended:

Theme D:

French horns and muted violas:

L'istesso tempo

A codetta using a fragment of theme C ends this section.

Section II—Tempest of Life

This section depicts a storm scene and is scherzo-like in character.

Theme E:

Allegro

The basic motive is developed followed by a statement of theme C.

Section III—Consolation of Nature

Basic Forms in Music

This section parallels in a sense the slow movement (lyric) of a symphony. A new theme is introduced by the clarinet and is used antiphonally by the strings and woodwinds.

Theme F:

A climax follows, built around Theme D.

Section IV—Struggle and Victory
Theme G:
Played by horns and trumpets:

Unity is enhanced by the return of theme D (in duple meter) and themes C and B.

ADDITIONAL EXAMPLES OF THE SYMPHONIC POEM

1. Sibelius, *Finlandia.*
2. Strauss, *Don Juan.*
3. Strauss, *Till Eulenspiegel.*
4. Smetana, *Ma Vlast* ("My Fatherland").
5. Saint-Saens, *Danse Macabre.*
6. Moussorgsky, *Night on Bald Mountain.*
7. Respighi, *Fountains of Rome.*
8. Debussy, *La Mer.*
9. Dukas, *L'Apprenti sorcier.*
10. Debussy, *L'Après-midi d'un Faune.*
11. Honegger, *Pacific 231.*
12. Stravinsky, *Fireworks.*
13. Rachmaninoff, *Isle of the Dead.*
14. Schoenberg, *Verklarte Nacht* ("Transfigured Night").
15. Gershwin, *An American in Paris.*
16. Sibelius, *Swan of Tuonela.*

This symphonic poem depicts the swan who floats and sings on the river which separates the land of the living from that of the dead, which is known in Finnish mythology as Tuonela. Its general mood is sad and wistful.

The Suite

THE BAROQUE SUITE

The Baroque suite originated in the lute music of the sixteenth and seventeenth centuries. It consists of a series of dances, usually in the same key and contrasting in tempo and meter. Each of the movements is usually in binary form (AB), with both sections similar in length or with the second section somewhat expanded, foreshadowing the sonata idea. The standard movements of the suite established by Bach are the allemande, courante, sarabande, and gigue. Several other dances are sometimes inserted between the sarabande and the gigue. These are the minuet, gavotte, bourrée, etc., which are usually song form and trio in design. Occasionally, the suite will begin with a prelude and will include a lyric movement, called an air.

Bach's *English Suite No. 2 in A Minor* for Harpsichord illustrates the Baroque suite.

Prelude

Allemande
4/4 meter, moderato, sixteenth-note upbeat

Courante
Triple meter, allegro, eighth-note upbeat

Sarabande
Slow dance in triple meter with a characteristic accent on the second beat of the measure

Bourřee I
Allegro, 4/4 meter with the characteristic rhythm

Bourřee II
   This alternative bourree is similar to a trio section. It is often
called a musette because of the bagpipe effect of the pedal or organ
point

Gigue
Presto, compound triple meter

The concerto grosso is a Baroque composition using a small group of solo instruments against a full orchestra (tutti) antiphonally. It was one of the new forms that developed with the great surge of instrumental music in the Baroque period. The movements usually alternate between rapid polyphonic movement and slower ones in chordal and homophonic style.

Examples of the concerto grosso are: Handel, *Concerto Grosso* Op. 13 Nos. 1 to 6; Corelli, *"Christmas" Concerto;* Bach, *Brandenburg Concerto No. 5 in D Major;* Bloch, *Concerto Grosso for Piano and String Orchestra.*

THE MODERN SUITE

The connecting link between the Baroque suite and the modern suite is the Classical divertimento, or serenade, which consists of a series of movements patterned after the sonata form. The movements vary in number and include dance forms and the basic forms of the sonata. The *Eine Kleine Nachtmusik* of Mozart is a typical example of this type of composition. It was written for string orchestra and is a miniature symphony in organization.

Several types of suites appeared in the nineteenth and twentieth centuries. These are (1) the ballet suite composed of excerpts from an original stage work, (2) the type which combines elements from the symphony and symphonic poem, and (3) the suite for solo instrument. The example below illustrates the first type.

Kodaly, *Hary Janos Suite*

This suite is derived from Kodaly's comic opera. The story is concerned with a character (Hary Janos) of Hungarian folklore who sits in the village and tells exaggerated stories of his great exploits. There are five sections to the suite, and the first two are presented here.

Section I

The form is free; unity is achieved by the repetition of the theme (the first three measures particularly) and variety by its transformation, alteration, and changes in instrumentation.

The main theme appears in the low strings, is imitated in the upper strings and bassoon, and builds to a considerable climax. The skip of the fourth, the outline of the triad, and the rhythmic pattern of the first three measures become important figures for the entire section.

Theme:

The theme appears in the first violins and is extended:

The theme is played in octaves by the flutes and strings. Notice the contrary motion.

Over soft sixteenth-note figures in the woodwinds and chords in the piano, the theme appears again, somewhat altered:

A short codetta presents the theme in another "variation:"

Section II—Viennese Musical Clock

Hary Janos becomes fascinated with a musical clock as its puppets appear and disappear. In contrast to the free form of Section I, this section is a clear and regular rondo form.

Part A:

Part B:

Part A returns
Part C:

Part A returns
Part D:

Return of part A closes the section.

ADDITIONAL EXAMPLES OF THE MODERN SUITE

1. Grieg, *Peer Gynt Suite Op. 46 No. 1.*
2. Saint-Saens, *Carnival des Animaux.*
3. Tschaikowsky, *Sleeping Beauty Op. 66.*
4. De Falla, *Three-Cornered Hat.*
5. Prokofiev, *Peter and the Wolf.*
6. Holst, *The Planets.*
7. Grofé, *Grand Canyon Suite.*
8. Stravinsky, *Petrouchka.*
9. Stravinsky, *The Fire Bird.*
10. Stravinsky, *Le Sacre du Printemps.*
11. Debussy, *La Mer.*
12. Debussy, *Nocturnes.*
13. Bizet, *L'Arlesienne Suite.*
14. Ravel, *Daphnis et Chloe Suites Nos. 1* and *2.*
15. Moussorgsky, *Pictures at an Exhibition.*

This suite was originally written for the piano and was later transcribed for orchestra by Ravel. Moussorgsky gives his musical impressions of 10 pictures from an exhibition of watercolors by his artist friend, V. Hartmann. The opening section and the interludes consist of a theme and variations, called Promenade, which represents the composer strolling from picture to picture in the art gallery.

The other themes are:
"The Gnome" (two contrasting melodies)
"The Old Castle"
"Tuilleries"—children disputing at their play
"Polish Wagon"—with enormous wheels
"Ballet of Chickens in Their Shells"
"Polish Jews"—one rich, the other poor
"Market Women"
"Catacombs"
"The Hut of Fowls Legs"
"The Great Gate at Kiev"

THE FANTASIA (FANTASIE)

The basic idea of the fantasia is a composition in an improvisational style using "the free light of fantasy." It is a style of composition rather than a form, has no formal organizational scheme, and is usually sectional in structure. Throughout all periods of music, composers have used this term in a number of ways. Several uses of the term are given here:

1. An early contrapuntal piece resembling a free fugue in the seventeenth century.

2. An improvisational-type composition preceding a fugue.

3. A series of themes or melodies from an opera.

4. The development section from a movement of a sonata is sometimes called a fantasia section.

5. An independent composition quite free in design and following no set pattern.

A unique composition is the *Fantasia on One Note* by Purcell. The tone middle C is sustained throughout the entire composition in the viola part while the other four instruments move in various harmonic and melodic patterns. A motive in stepwise movement is imitated in the various voices at the beginning:

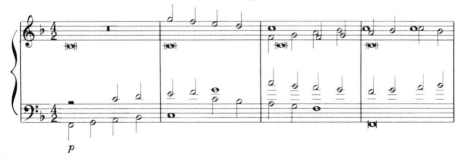

The motive is heard again, this time in quarter- and eighth-note movement. After a short interlude in minor, a fugal section appears with the use of this motive:

The last few measures offer a homophonic close to the composition.

The second example of the fantasia is the Vaughan Williams *Fantasia on a Theme by Thomas Tallis*. It is scored for string quartet and double string orchestra and is heard in several sections.

Section I

The music begins with a series of chords in contrary motion:

The initial motive from the theme appears in the low register against a sustained D in the upper strings, followed by a series of parallel chords. These chords are used as interludes and as an antiphonal device throughout the composition.

The theme is then stated in full:

Section II

The solo viola presents a theme derived from the second part of the Tallis theme. It is taken up by the solo violin and is used imitatively by the solo quartet. The orchestra supplies the interlude material consisting of a series of chords:

Section III

Fragments of the melody appear in various combinations in this development section.

Section IV

An extended passage opening with the theme in the solo violin, with the viola offering a counter melody, is followed by a coda using the series of chords again.

EXAMPLES OF THE FANTASIA

1. Bach, *Fantasia and Fugue in G minor* for Organ.
2. Bach, *Chromatic Fantasia and Fugue in D minor.*
3. Mozart, *Fantasia in D minor K.397.*
4. Mozart, *Fantasia in C minor, K.475.*
5. Beethoven, *Choral Fantasy for Piano, Chorus, and Orchestra.*
6. Schubert, *Wanderer Fantasie for Piano.*
7. Schumann, *Fantasia in C major for Piano.*

8. Chopin, *Fantasie-Impromptu Op. 66.*
9. Chopin, *Fantasie in F minor Op. 49.*
10. Weber, *Hungarian Fantasie for Bassoon.*
11. Vaughan Williams, *Fantasia on Greensleeves.*
12. Britten, *Fantasy Quartet.*

Composers through the years have used a number of different terms for independent compositions—rhapsody, capriccio, intermezzo, toccata, scherzo, etude, etc. The form of these compositions may closely follow one of the basic forms; it may be modified in some way; or it may be free and unconventional in its organization and structure. Even though certain titles have general connotations—capriccio usually indicates a quick tempo; toccata (to touch), a free improvisational style with running scale passages and chords; and the etude, consisting of one motive from which the whole piece grows and demonstrates a particular technical problem—they are often used interchangeably and follow no set design or pattern.

List

of

Musical

Examples

Basic Forms in Music

Basic Forms in Music

Basic Forms in Music

General

Index